TRY
JESUS

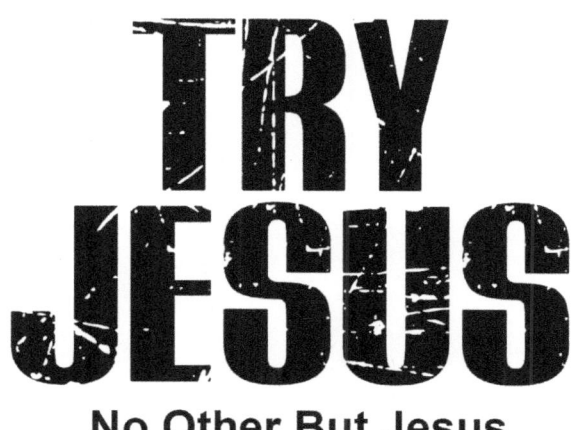

No Other But Jesus

NANA-SEI TWERETWIE

TRY JESUS: NO OTHER BUT JESUS

© 2025 by Rev. Nana-Sei Tweretwie

All rights reserved. No part of this book may be reproduced or transmitted in any form or by any means, electronic or mechanical, including photocopying, recording, or by any information storage and retrieval system, without prior written permission of the author and/or publisher, except where permitted by law.

Contact the Author via:
tweretwienana70@gmail.com

PUBLISHED BY

Tweretwie Ministries
Milton Keynes
United Kingdom

DEDICATION

I dedicate this book to the glory of God, whose grace and wisdom have guided every word written within these pages. To Jesus Christ, the source of all wisdom, knowledge and truth, whose love and sacrifice have been the foundation of my faith and inspiration. I also dedicate this work to the Holy Spirit, who has given me strength, in-depth understanding, many revelations, and the power to accomplish this glorious work. Again, to those seeking a deeper relationship with the Lord, especially the Body of Christ, and those who are ordained for eternal life yet have not received the Lord. I pray that these words of wisdom lead you closer to the Lord and fill your life with His unending peace, joy and wisdom to fulfil His divine purpose in life. May this book serve as a beacon of hope and light for all who read it, in Jesus' Mighty Name. Amen!

"An excellent future must begin with Christ Jesus, for without Christ, there is no future."

CONTENTS

Dedication v

Acknowledgement xiii

Introduction xv

CHAPTER ONE
A World of Uncertainty 1

    Embracing Faith in a World of Uncertainty 3

    Trusting Jesus in Uncertain Times 5

    Trusting Jesus in Every Season of Life 7

    Note these 9

    The Urgent Need to Trust Jesus in a Time of Spiritual Famine 9

    Trusting Jesus: The Anchor in a World of Spiritual Famine 11

    Jesus, The Everlasting Source of Living Water 12

    Note these 14

    Faith in Christ: Anchored in Uncertainty 15

CHAPTER TWO
The World in the Time of Noah: A Mirror for Our Generation 17

    Note these 19

    A Call to Trust in Jesus 19

    The Silence of God and Personal Salvation 21

    The Individual Nature of Faith 23

Note these 25
The Family Saved by Faith 25
Salvation Through Obedience and Faith 27
A World in Darkness: The Need for Spiritual Awakening 29
Note these 31

CHAPTER THREE

Light in the Darkness 33
The Reality of Hardship 34
Find Strength and Peace in Jesus 36
Embrace the End with Jesus 38
Jesus, God's Redemption and the Path to New Beginnings 39
Note these 42

CHAPTER FOUR

The Reality of Spiritual Battles 43
Victory Through Christ in Spiritual Battles 44
The Struggle Between Light and Darkness 47
Note these 49
Jesus Our Defender in Battle 49
Trying Jesus: The Path to Spiritual Victory 51
Note these 53

CHAPTER FIVE

Jesus, the Answer to Life's Burdens 55
Jesus, The Only Sure Foundation 57
Note these 58
A Mighty Man in Need of Jesus 59

Note these 60

The Power of Humility in Receiving God's Blessings 60

Note these 62

CHAPTER SIX

Wealth and Power Could Not Bring True Healing 63

Humility and Obedience Lead to God's Blessings 65

Note these 67

No One is Safe Without Jesus 67

Healing from the Leprosy of Life 68

Jesus Cleanses the "Leprosy" of Sin 70

The Hidden Leprosy in Our Lives 72

Only Jesus Can Heal the Hidden Leprosy 73

Note these 75

CHAPTER SEVEN

The Illusion of Success without Jesus 77

Obey His Word 78

A Call to Surrender to Jesus Christ 80

Note these 82

Jesus Will Carry Your Burdens 82

Jesus Will Give You Rest 83

Trust in Jesus Completely 85

Note these 87

CHAPTER EIGHT

Jesus is Able to Deliver You 89

Push Through Faith 91

Seize the Moment: Call on Jesus Before It's Too Late 92
Note these 94
Break Free from Every Stronghold 94
Jesus Breaks Every Curse and Barrier 96
He Breaks Every Curse and Barrier 98
Note these 100

CHAPTER NINE
Don't Sit Back and Watch – Take Action 101
Note these 103
God has the Power to Silence the Devil 103
Note these 105
These Are Not Just Stories – They Are Real 105
Faith Over Expectations 107
Human Expectations and God's Divine Ways 108
Faith Is the Key to Miracles 110
Note these 112
Don't Reject God Because of Human Logic 112
Note these 114

CHAPTER TEN
He Knows the Way 115
Trusting God Beyond Your Expectations 117
God does not Work According to our Expectations 118
Note these 120
Generational Problems Need a Spiritual Solution 121
Stop Making Life Harder Than It Should Be 122
Note these 124

CHAPTER ELEVEN

Break the Cycle: Stand for Your Family *125*

   Stand with God for Your Family 126

   Break the Cycle of Ignorance and Regret 128

   Note these 130

   Recognize and Destroy Spiritual Decay 130

   Restoration from Spiritual Brokenness 132

   Greatness Can Often Be Overshadowed by Hidden Struggles 133

   Note these 135

Conclusion *137*

References *139*

Bible References *147*

Other books by the Author *151*

Author's Profile *153*

ACKNOWLEDGEMENT

My deepest gratitude goes to God the Father, our Lord Jesus Christ, and the Holy Spirit, who have made me who I am today. Without His mercies and grace, I could not have come this far.

I am profoundly thankful to my wife, Rev. Mrs Yvonne Tweretwie, and our children, Cecilia Kyeretwie, Emmanuel Tweretwie, David Tweretwie, Samuel Tweretwie and Joseph Tweretwie for their unwavering love and tremendous support.

I extend heartfelt appreciation to Rev. Prof. Nana Kyei-Baffour, Healthcare Chaplain, Course Director of Postgraduate Education in Healthcare Chaplaincy, Adjunct Professor with Global University (Assemblies of God, USA), and Senior Pastor at Victory-City Assemblies of God, Wallington-London. He is an extraordinary mentor who consistently goes the extra mile to guide me in the right direction. May the Lord Almighty richly bless you for your invaluable presence in my life.

Not forgetting my Senior Pastor, Rev. Collins Okai, at Gospel Light Assemblies of God Church, Kumasi, Ghana, who nurtured me in my Christian life and walk with God.

Kudos to my spiritual children in the Lord, Vincent Eloh, Clifford Adom, Josephine Osei, Comfort Adusei, and Juliet Adusei, who are working tirelessly and immensely to advance this glorious assignment the Lord has given me.

Finally, I deeply cherish the love and support from the family of Miracle Temple Assemblies of God Church (MTAG), Milton Keynes, United Kingdom. Words cannot fully express my gratitude to them; their kindness and encouragement mean the world to me.

INTRODUCTION

In today's fast-paced and ever-changing world, countless individuals, including some Christians, struggle with doubt when it comes to the miracles, power, and favor of Jesus Christ. Many question whether involving Jesus in their daily lives, businesses, marriages, health, struggles, and personal plans truly makes a difference. This uncertainty stems from a culture that often seeks quick solutions through human wisdom while sidelining the divine. Yet, the Bible reminds us in Jeremiah 33:3 (NIV), *"Call to me and I will answer you and tell you great and unsearchable things you do not know."* This book, *TRY JESUS: NO OTHER BUT JESUS*, invites every reader to reconsider could the answer you've been seeking all along be found in Jesus?

Despite the incredible advancements in science, technology, and human knowledge, humanity is still confronted with unexplainable mysteries and deep questions about existence, purpose, and destiny. Modern discoveries have opened galaxies, connected nations, and extended life expectancy, but none of these advancements have solved the longing in the human heart for true peace, meaning, and hope. As Psalm 145:3 (NIV) declares, *"Great is the Lord and most worthy of praise; his greatness no one can fathom."* No human achievement can replace the wisdom and power of the Creator Himself. This reality forms a foundation for *TRY JESUS*, as it challenges readers to step beyond human understanding and into divine revelation.

At the core of this book is the urgent call to recognize the supremacy and authority of Jesus Christ over every area of life. Jesus is not just a religious figure to admire from a distance. He is the Light of the world, the Savior of souls, and the One who holds power over life and death. In John 8:12 (NIV), Jesus boldly proclaims, *"I am the light of the world. Whoever follows me will never walk in darkness, but will have the light of life."* This book encourages every reader to pause and reflect, what if the answers you need, the strength you lack, and the hope you crave are all found in Jesus?

With this in mind, *Try Jesus* has been prayerfully written as a spiritual manual and guide to open hearts to the transformative power of Christ. Drawing from philosophical insights, deep biblical truths, and scholarly research, the book breaks down why trying Jesus is not only important but absolutely necessary for a fulfilled life. As Proverbs 3:5-6 (NIV) urges, *"Trust in the Lord with all your heart and lean not on your own understanding; in all your ways submit to him, and he will make your paths straight."* Every chapter unfolds practical wisdom and timeless truth designed to shift your perspective and ignite your faith.

The book is structured into eleven enlightening chapters, each addressing critical aspects of life where Jesus offers answers the world cannot. Topics such as navigating uncertainty, overcoming spiritual battles, healing from life's burdens, and breaking destructive cycles are explored in depth. Every page aims to stir your spirit, renew your mind, and point you to the hope found in Jesus Christ alone. As you read *Try Jesus*, I encourage you not just to skim the pages but to meditate and seek God's voice through them. May James 1:22 (NIV) be your guide: *"Do not merely listen to the word, and so deceive yourselves. Do what it says."* My prayer is that this book becomes not just information, but a divine invitation to encounter the living Christ in a deeper, more personal way. God richly bless you as you begin this journey.

CHAPTER ONE

A WORLD OF UNCERTAINTY

The world, as described, is a vast, dynamic system shaped by nature, human societies, cultures, technologies, and cosmic events, yet despite human advancements, there remains much we do not know. Science explores the galaxies, medicine unlocks biological mysteries, and technology connects the globe, but can humanity ever fully comprehend the workings of creation? The Bible reminds us of our limited understanding when it says, *"Great is the Lord and most worthy of praise; his greatness no one can fathom."* (Psalm 145:3, NIV). This reminds believers that while humans seek knowledge, ultimate understanding belongs to God alone. Max Lucado once said, "Feed your fears, and your faith will starve. Feed your faith, and your fears will." This quote highlights the importance of nurturing faith to diminish fear's influence.

Uncertainty is not just a scientific or economic reality, it is also a spiritual one. The future, personal decisions, relationships, and even life itself are unpredictable. James 4:14 (NIV) asks, *"Why, you do not even know what will happen tomorrow. What is your life? You are a mist that appears for a little while and then vanishes."* This biblical truth humbles humanity, reminding us that control is an illusion. Yet, this very uncertainty drives believers toward dependence on God. C.S. Lewis wrote, *"The great thing, if one can, is to stop regarding all the unpleasant things as interruptions of one's 'own,' or 'real' life. The truth is, of course that what one calls the interruptions are precisely one's real life the life God is sending one day by day."* In other words, uncertainty is not an obstacle to faith, but a stage upon which faith is built.

Throughout history, biblical figures faced uncertainty and found hope in God's promises. Abraham left his homeland without knowing his destination (Hebrews 11:8, Niv), **and the Israelites wandered the desert for 40 years without clear answers about the future, yet God's presence guided them. What does this teach us? It reveals that uncertainty is often God's tool for refining faith and character.** Proverbs 3:5-6 (Niv) advises, *"Trust in the Lord with all your heart and lean not on your own understanding; in all your ways submit to him, and he will make your paths straight."* This does not eliminate uncertainty but offers divine direction within it. As Oswald Chambers wrote, *"Faith never knows where it is being led, but it loves and knows the One who is leading."* This mindset allows believers to walk confidently even in times of global crisis, personal trials, or economic instability.

In a modern world filled with economic instability, climate crises, technological shifts, and pandemics, uncertainty is not a passing phase but our reality. **How should individuals and societies respond? First, by acknowledging that human control is limited, and second, by embracing adaptability, innovation, and trust in God.** Matthew 6:34 (Niv) teaches, *"Therefore do not worry about tomorrow, for tomorrow will worry about itself. Each day has enough trouble of its own."* This is not a call to ignorance but to faith-filled stewardship, which means taking wise action today while trusting God for the future. This lesson is crucial for leaders, youth, and families alike: uncertainty is not an enemy to fear, but an opportunity to deepen faith and build resilience.

For future generations, the reality of uncertainty will only intensify as global challenges become more complex, and what legacy should today's Christians leave behind? A legacy of faith over fear, wisdom over panic, and hope over despair. Ecclesiastes 11:5 (Niv) declares, *"As you do not know the path of the wind, or how the body is formed in a mother's womb, so you cannot understand the work of God, the Maker of all things."* Teaching children and youth to embrace life's uncertainties with faith, critical thinking, and adaptability prepares them for a future where change is the only constant. Dietrich Bonhoeffer wrote, "The essence of optimism is not blindly ignoring the present but a source of inspiration that never abandons hope." By grounding the next generation in both spiritual faith and practical wisdom, believers ensure that uncertainty becomes a path to growth, not fear, leaving them with the courage to face whatever lies ahead.

EMBRACING FAITH IN A WORLD OF UNCERTAINTY

A world of uncertainty reflects the reality that human beings, despite their careful planning and pursuit of control, ultimately live in an unpredictable environment where the future is never fully known. People set goals, build careers, and plan for their families, yet life's unexpected twists, natural disasters, economic collapses, personal losses, and global crises frequently remind us that control is fleeting. The Bible acknowledges this human limitation in *Ecclesiastes 8:7 (NIV)*, which states, *"Since no one knows the future, who can tell someone else what is to come?"* **This raises a rhetorical question for all generations: If no one can predict or control the future, where should we place our trust?** Some may lean on technology, scientific advancement, or strategic foresight, yet these tools, as powerful as they are, remain limited. As Oswald Chambers observed, "Faith never knows where it is being led, but it loves and knows the One who is leading." In other words, it is not about having perfect knowledge of the future but having complete confidence in God's leadership.

Uncertainty stirs deep emotions such as fear, anxiety, and doubt because human nature craves security and predictability. In areas like finances, career paths, and even relationships, the desire for certainty can lead to hesitation, over-planning, or paralyzing fear. Yet, Jesus challenges this mindset in *Matthew 6:34 (NIV)* when He says, *"Therefore do not worry about tomorrow, for tomorrow will worry about itself. Each day has enough trouble of its own."* This teaching does not dismiss the reality of uncertainty but instead calls believers to a life of daily dependence on God. The great Christian thinker C.S. Lewis captured this tension when he wrote, "Relying on God has to begin all over again every day as if nothing had yet been done." Thus, rather than allowing fear to govern their decisions, Christians are called to practice daily trust, knowing that God holds both the present and the future in His hands.

While some see uncertainty as a source of fear, others view it as an invitation to grow spiritually, emotionally, and intellectually. The unpredictable nature of life can lead to innovation, discovery, and deepening personal faith. In James 1:2-4 (NIV), the Bible says, *"Consider it pure joy, my brothers and sisters, whenever you face trials of many kinds, because you know that the testing of your faith produces perseverance."* This perspective challenges the human tendency to resist discomfort and uncertainty. When people shift from fearing the unknown to embracing it as an opportunity for growth, they develop resilience and wisdom. Saint Augustine once said, "Trust the past to the mercy of God, the present to His love, and the future to His providence." Augustine's words remind us to entrust every aspect of our lives to God, finding peace in His mercy, love, and providential care.

Uncertainty will continue to define life on Earth for future generations, but how they respond will shape their spiritual journeys and life outcomes. Rather than fearing change, young people should be taught to embrace faith-based adaptability learning to trust God's guidance while using their gifts and knowledge to address life's challenges. Proverbs 3:5-6 (NIV) offers timeless wisdom: *"Trust in the Lord with all your heart and lean not on your own understanding; in all your ways submit to him, and he will make your paths straight."* This is more than a call to religious devotion; it is an invitation to live wisely and courageously. The greatest lesson believers can pass down is that faith does not remove uncertainty, but it does transform it from an enemy to fear into a journey to embrace. By teaching future generations to trust God, think critically, and act wisely, Christians prepare them not just to survive uncertainty but to thrive within it, becoming strong leaders grounded in faith and equipped to serve in a complex and changing world.

TRUSTING JESUS IN UNCERTAIN TIMES

Trusting Jesus in uncertain times is not a passive act of hoping for the best, but an intentional decision to rely on His wisdom, power, and love when life becomes unpredictable. **Human beings naturally seek stability through careful planning, financial security, or personal achievements, yet these efforts often fall short when unexpected challenges arise.** Jesus Himself acknowledged the inevitability of uncertainty in *John 16:33 (NIV)* when He said, *"In this world you will have trouble. But take heart! I have overcome the world."* This statement does not promise a life free from difficulties but offers the assurance that Jesus has ultimate authority over all situations. Can human wisdom truly guarantee lasting peace, or is there a greater peace found in trusting the One who holds all of creation in His hands?

In times of uncertainty, believers are reminded that Jesus is not only aware of their struggles but also fully able to guide them through. As the Son of God, Jesus possesses both divine knowledge and compassion, making Him the perfect source of comfort and direction. *Matthew 6:8 (NIV)* affirms this by declaring, *"Your Father knows what you need before you ask him."* This profound truth should prompt reflection: If God already knows our needs, why do we still fear the unknown? Instead of being paralyzed by uncertainty, believers are invited to rest in the assurance that Jesus walks ahead of them, preparing the way. R.c. Sproul, *Does God Control Everything? "If God is not sovereign, God is not God. If there is even one maverick molecule in the universe, one molecule running loose outside the scope of God's sovereign ordination, we cannot have the slightest confidence that any promise God has ever made about the future will come to pass."* Trusting Jesus does not mean ignoring reality or pretending life is easy; it means choosing faith over fear even when circumstances remain unclear. The ever-changing world, filled with political instability, economic shifts, and personal hardships, constantly reminds people of their limited control. Yet *Hebrews 13:8 (NIV)* declares, *"Jesus Christ is the same yesterday and today and forever."* This constancy in Christ offers a firm foundation in a world that constantly shifts beneath our feet. What if uncertainty is not meant to break us but to build us? What if uncertainty is God's way of teaching deeper reliance on Him? Oswald Chambers once said, *"Faith is deliberate confidence in the character of God whose ways you may not understand at the time."* In trusting Jesus, believers transform uncertainty into an opportunity for spiritual growth and deeper intimacy with their Savior.

Prayer plays a vital role in nurturing this trust, as it shifts focus away from personal fear and toward divine peace. Through prayer, believers actively surrender their worries to Jesus, choosing to believe that His wisdom surpasses their understanding. *Philippians 4:6-7 (NIV)* encourages this practice, stating, *"Do not be anxious about anything, but in every situation, by prayer and petition, with thanksgiving, present your requests to God. And the peace of God, which transcends all understanding, will guard your hearts and minds in Christ Jesus."* Does prayer instantly remove uncertainty? Not always, but it realigns the believer's perspective, replacing panic with peace and fear with faith.

For both current and future generations, trusting Jesus in uncertain times offers invaluable lessons. It teaches that faith is not about having all the answers but trusting the One who does. It reminds believers that peace does not come from perfect circumstances but from perfect confidence in God's sovereignty. As the world faces growing complexities, climate crises, technological upheavals, and social uncertainty, the need for faith in Jesus becomes even more urgent. *Proverbs 3:5-6 (NIV)* offers timeless guidance: *"Trust in the Lord with all your heart and lean not on your own understanding; in all your ways submit to him, and he will make your paths straight."* This verse is more than a comforting quote; it is a call to action. By trusting Jesus through prayer, obedience, and meditation on Scripture, believers gain the spiritual resilience to face any uncertainty with courage and hope. This legacy of trust is one of the greatest gifts the current generation can pass on to the next.

TRUSTING JESUS IN EVERY SEASON OF LIFE

Trusting Jesus is not limited to moments of crisis; it is a lifelong invitation to walk in faith through every season, whether joyful or challenging, clear or confusing. **In the mundane routines of life, it can be easy to rely on personal strength or daily habits, forgetting the importance of trusting in Christ. Yet, Jesus calls His followers to surrender their fears and uncertainties to Him daily, not just when difficulties arise.** *Matthew 6:34 (NIV)* reminds believers, *"Therefore do not worry about tomorrow, for tomorrow will worry about itself. Each day has enough trouble of its own."* This instruction shifts the focus from obsessing over the unknown future to trusting God's provision for today. Can anyone truly predict tomorrow's events with certainty? If human wisdom is so limited, does it not make sense to trust the One who knows the end from the beginning? Max Lucado states, "Feed your fears and your faith will starve. Feed your faith, and your fears will starve."

In times of major life transitions, whether through career shifts, personal loss, or unexpected changes, trusting Jesus becomes a vital anchor. Human plans, no matter how carefully crafted, often encounter unexpected detours. Yet *Proverbs 16:9 (NIV)* teaches, *"In their hearts humans plan their course, but the Lord establishes their steps."* This verse highlights the divine interplay between human effort and God's ultimate authority. **How often do people find themselves frustrated when their plans fall apart, only to later realize God was redirecting them to something better?** Elisabeth Elliot, a well-known Christian author, wrote, "God never withholds from His child that which His love and wisdom call good." This truth invites believers to view life's interruptions not as obstacles, but as opportunities to trust in God's higher plan.

Even in prolonged seasons of uncertainty such as waiting for answers, recovering from heartbreak, or facing health challenges, Jesus offers Himself as a constant source of comfort and strength. *Isaiah 41:10 (NIV)* reassures, *"So do not fear, for I am with you; do not be dismayed, for I am your God."* This divine promise offers not just hope for the future, but strength for the present. What gives greater peace, trusting in temporary solutions or trusting in the eternal Savior who walks beside us? Corrie ten Boom famously said, "Never be afraid to trust an unknown future to a known God." This shift in mindset allows believers to replace fear of the unknown with confidence in God's unfailing presence.

Trusting Jesus also transforms the way believers interpret hardships. Instead of viewing suffering as pointless pain, faith sees trials as opportunities for growth and deeper reliance on Christ. James 1:2-3 (NIV) instructs, *"Consider it pure joy, my brothers and sisters, whenever you face trials of many kinds, because you know that the testing of your faith produces perseverance."* This perspective invites Christians to ask themselves: What if uncertainty is not meant to destroy faith, but to deepen it? What if moments of confusion are divine invitations to seek God's wisdom more intentionally? Oswald Chambers wrote, "Faith never knows where it is being led, but it loves and knows the One who is leading." Such trust produces endurance and resilience that can only be forged through seasons of challenge.

For both current and future generations, trusting Jesus in every season offers timeless lessons. It teaches that faith is not about securing easy outcomes, but about leaning on the unchanging character of God in a constantly changing world. It challenges believers to cultivate a daily habit of surrender through prayer, obedience, and reflection on God's Word so that trust in Christ becomes second nature, not just a crisis response. In an era marked by global uncertainty, political instability, and personal struggles, future generations must learn that true security is not found in wealth, power, or technology but in the presence of Jesus Himself. *Psalm 125:1 (NIV)* declares, *"Those who trust in the Lord are like Mount Zion, which cannot be shaken but endures forever."* This enduring trust is the spiritual inheritance every generation should strive to pass on to the next.

NOTE THESE

1. True security comes from trusting Jesus, not from human plans or understanding.
2. Every season of life, whether joyful or challenging, is an opportunity to grow in faith.
3. God's plans are often different from human expectations, but they always lead to purpose and good.
4. Prayer, obedience, and meditation on God's Word help believers trust Jesus daily.
5. Trusting Jesus transforms uncertainty from a source of fear into a journey of spiritual growth.

THE URGENT NEED TO TRUST JESUS IN A TIME OF SPIRITUAL FAMINE

The prophecy in Amos 8:11 paints a sobering picture of a coming famine not of physical bread or water, but of hearing the Word of God. This spiritual famine reflects a time when people no longer desire or value divine truth, drifting instead into moral confusion and spiritual blindness. In today's rapidly changing world, we can already observe signs of this famine as society increasingly distances itself from biblical teachings and the pursuit of God's wisdom. **When divine truth is no longer the foundation of life, people are left to wander in darkness, making decisions based on personal desires and cultural trends rather than God's eternal principles.** Is it any wonder that anxiety, depression, and hopelessness have become so widespread? In the face of such spiritual drought, trusting Jesus becomes essential. As the Living Word (John 1:1), Jesus offers the very truth and life that humanity desperately needs.

This famine is not caused by the physical absence of Bibles or the closing of churches. Rather, it arises when people lose their hunger for God's Word and become indifferent to its truth. In an age of overwhelming information, countless voices demand attention, yet the one voice that truly matters, the voice of God, gets drowned out. Society teaches that wealth, success, and self-fulfillment bring ultimate satisfaction, but these pursuits often leave people feeling empty and directionless. Francis Chan, Crazy Love: Overwhelmed by a Relentless God once wrote, "God is the treasure, and where the treasure is, there is the heart. By this we may test our love to God." When people turn from God's truth, their hearts become spiritually malnourished, longing for purpose yet refusing the very bread that gives life (John 6:35). What would happen if people truly believed that man does not live by bread alone, but by every word that comes from the mouth of God (Matthew 4:4)?

The Word of God was always meant to serve as a guiding light for humanity, illuminating the right path in a dark world. Psalm 119:105 declares, *"Your word is a lamp for my feet, a light on my path."* When people neglect this divine light, they stumble into confusion, no longer able to discern right from wrong. This drift away from God rarely happens instantly; it is often the result of gradual compromise. When prayer is neglected, Scripture is ignored, and obedience is replaced by self-will, the heart becomes hardened and resistant to divine truth. Paul warned in 2 Timothy 4:3-4 that a time would come when people would turn away from sound doctrine, preferring teachings that align with their desires rather than God's will. What happens to a society that prioritizes comfort over truth? It falls into spiritual starvation, and no amount of technology, education, or wealth can fill that void.

For both current and future generations, this message holds critical lessons. First, spiritual hunger can only be satisfied by the Bread of Life, Jesus Himself. Second, believers must remain anchored in God's Word, guarding their hearts against the subtle drift toward spiritual indifference. Third, trusting Jesus requires the active pursuit of His truth, not a passive acceptance of comfortable lies. Charles Spurgeon once said, *"A Bible that's falling apart usually belongs to someone who isn't."* This is a call for today's believers to immerse themselves in Scripture, knowing that Jesus alone provides the truth that sustains life. When the famine of the Word comes, only those who have hidden God's Word in their hearts (Psalm 119:11) will stand firm, becoming lights in the darkness and pointing others to the eternal truth found in Jesus Christ.

TRUSTING JESUS: THE ANCHOR IN A WORLD OF SPIRITUAL FAMINE

In times of uncertainty and moral decline, trusting Jesus becomes not just a spiritual option, but an urgent necessity. As the living Word, He embodies divine truth and the fulfillment of God's promises. His teachings bring light to a world consumed by confusion and deception. Without Jesus, people are left searching for answers in places that cannot satisfy the soul. Can temporary pleasures, wealth, or human philosophies truly replace the eternal wisdom of Christ? Proverbs 3:5-6 (NIV) reminds believers to, *"Trust in the Lord with all your heart and lean not on your own understanding; in all your ways submit to him, and he will make your paths straight."* When human understanding falls short, Jesus becomes the only sure foundation, one who does not change with cultural trends, but stands as the eternal source of stability and truth.

Even in the midst of spiritual famine, hope still exists for those who trust in Jesus. In John 6:35 (NIV), Jesus declares, *"I am the bread of life. Whoever comes to me will never go hungry, and whoever believes in me will never be thirsty."* This powerful statement reveals that Jesus alone satisfies the deep hunger for meaning, purpose, and spiritual fulfillment. While the world promotes self-reliance and independence, the truth is that true peace comes from dependence on Christ. Practical examples of this truth are evident throughout history. During the Great Depression, countless families lost everything, yet testimonies emerged of those who, despite having no material wealth, found peace and purpose in Jesus. What allowed them to endure while others gave in to despair? It was their trust in the One who provides eternal nourishment, not temporary relief.

Now is the moment to hunger for God's Word and seek Jesus with sincere hearts. The longer one delays, the harder it becomes to recognize the spiritual famine within. Just as prolonged physical starvation dulls the appetite, spiritual neglect numbs the heart to God's voice. Yet God's promise in Jeremiah 29:13 (NIV) stands true: *"You will seek me and find me when you seek me with all your heart."* No one is beyond redemption, and no heart is too far gone. The story of the prodigal son in Luke 15 reminds us that God eagerly welcomes those who return to Him. Why risk allowing worldly distractions to drown out the still, small voice calling you back to truth? As Brother Lawrence, The Practice of the Presence of God, said, "There is not in the world a kind of life more sweet and delightful than that of a continual conversation with God." Seeking Jesus through prayer, Bible study, and obedience opens the door to personal revival, even when the world seems spiritually dry.

For both this generation and those to come, trusting Jesus in a time of famine teaches crucial lessons. First, no earthly success or wealth can replace spiritual fulfillment in Christ. Second, delaying to seek God only deepens spiritual hunger, making the heart vulnerable to deception. Third, God's Word remains the only reliable guide in uncertain times. Finally, trusting Jesus does not eliminate hardship, but it brings strength, peace, and purpose within the hardship. In a world starving for truth, Jesus offers eternal nourishment to all who will come to Him, making trust in Him not just important, but essential for survival, direction, and eternal hope.

JESUS, THE EVERLASTING SOURCE OF LIVING WATER

Jesus stands as the ultimate source of living water, offering spiritual nourishment that nothing in this world can provide. *In John 7:37-38 (NIV), Jesus stood and said in a loud voice, "Let anyone who is thirsty come to me and drink. Whoever believes in me, as Scripture has said, rivers of living water will flow from within them."* This invitation speaks to all who experience spiritual dryness, a condition where life feels empty, even when material needs are met. Can wealth, fame, or human relationships truly quench the deep thirst of the soul? The world offers temporary satisfaction, but only Jesus gives eternal fulfillment. Horatio Spafford, It Is Well with My Soul, wrote, "When peace like a river, attendeth my way, when sorrows like sea billows roll; whatever my lot, Thou hast taught me to say, it is well, it is well, with my soul." Those who drink from the living water of Christ discover a constant flow of peace, purpose, and guidance, even when life becomes uncertain.

Receiving this living water, however, demands more than just casual belief; it requires surrender, obedience, and a deep commitment to follow Jesus. Spiritual thirst can only be satisfied when believers seek God wholeheartedly, immerse themselves in His Word, and allow the Holy Spirit to guide every decision. *Psalm 1:3 (NIV) compares the faithful to a tree planted by streams of water, which yields fruit in season and whose leaf does not wither.* This imagery shows that those who root themselves in Christ, feeding on His truth, remain spiritually healthy even in times of drought. But what happens to those who neglect this living water? Can a tree survive long without a source of nourishment? Just as physical dehydration weakens the body, spiritual neglect leaves the soul vulnerable to doubt, temptation, and confusion.

This truth becomes even more critical during hardships, moments of doubt, and spiritual emptiness. In these difficult seasons, Jesus' invitation to receive rest and renewal becomes a lifeline. *Matthew 11:28 (NIV) declares, "Come to me, all you who are weary and burdened, and I will give you rest."* Whether facing personal trials, societal chaos, or moral decline, Jesus offers peace that surpasses understanding. A practical example can be seen in the life of Corrie ten Boom, who, even while imprisoned in a concentration camp, found peace and strength through her unwavering trust in Christ. She famously said, "You can never learn that Christ is all you need, until Christ is all you have." This kind of trust is only possible when believers drink deeply from the living water, allowing Christ to sustain them in every circumstance.

The consequences of ignoring this living water are visible today in a world experiencing spiritual barrenness. When people drift from God, hunger for His Word fades, and truth becomes optional rather than essential. *Amos 8:11 (NIV) warns, "The days are coming," declares the*

Sovereign Lord, "when I will send a famine through the land—not a famine of food or a thirst for water, but a famine of hearing the words of the Lord." This prophecy comes alive when churches prioritize entertainment over sound doctrine, when believers compromise biblical values for cultural acceptance, and when society replaces divine truth with personal opinions. In such a barren environment, deception thrives, and people chase after fleeting pleasures instead of eternal life.

For generations, several lessons have emerged from this reality. First, spiritual thirst can only be quenched by Jesus, not the temporary offerings of the world. Second, consistent immersion in God's Word keeps the living water flowing. Third, true fulfillment comes through surrender and obedience to Christ. Fourth, spiritual drought is dangerous, leading to moral decline and confusion. Finally, sharing the living water with others is essential, for what good is a well if no one drinks from it? Charles Spurgeon wisely stated, "Nobody ever outgrows Scripture; the book widens and deepens with our years." In every season, Jesus remains the faithful fountain, offering life-giving water to all who seek Him with sincere hearts.

NOTE THESE

1. True spiritual satisfaction comes only from Jesus, the living water, not from worldly success or pleasures.

2. Staying rooted in God's Word keeps believers strong and nourished, even in difficult times.

3. Ignoring God's truth leads to spiritual barrenness, confusion, and moral decay.

4. Trusting Jesus brings peace, guidance, and eternal purpose, even when life is uncertain.

5. Every believer has a responsibility to share the living water of Christ with others who are spiritually thirsty.

FAITH IN CHRIST: ANCHORED IN UNCERTAINTY

Life's uncertainties have a way of exposing the limits of human strength, wisdom, and resources. Economic instability, health crises, unexpected loss, and personal failures leave many feeling overwhelmed and disoriented. In such moments, Jesus stands as the unshakable anchor for the soul, offering a peace that transcends circumstances. *"Cast all your anxiety on him because he cares for you"* (1 Peter 5:7, NIV). Why do so many cling to fleeting security in wealth, careers, or personal connections when true peace comes only from Christ? Andrew Murray, Waiting on God, once wrote, "Faith expects from God what is beyond all expectation." Real faith in Jesus brings rest because it shifts the burden from human hands into divine ones, where every uncertainty is met with God's eternal faithfulness.

The reality of uncertainty is universal, no one is exempt from moments when life takes an unexpected turn. Plans crumble, relationships strain, and fears arise about the future. In such seasons, some try to rely on their intellect, making impulsive decisions driven by fear. But Scripture urges us to take a different approach: *"Trust in the Lord with all your heart and lean not on your own understanding"* (Proverbs 3:5, NIV). Is it not wiser to place our fragile lives in the hands of an unchanging God rather than trusting in our limited understanding? Faith in Jesus does not eliminate uncertainty, but it transforms it into an opportunity to witness His guidance and provision firsthand.

To place faith in Jesus is not a passive act, but a deliberate surrender that invites Him into every aspect of life. It means acknowledging personal weakness and embracing divine strength. Jesus Himself assures us of His unwavering nature: *"Jesus Christ is the same yesterday and today and forever"* (Hebrews 13:8, NIV). This truth offers incredible comfort when everything changes, He remains constant. Those who walk closely with Him can testify that even in their most difficult moments, His presence sustains them. Consider a practical example: a business owner facing bankruptcy may panic and take unethical shortcuts to stay afloat. However, a believer who trusts in Jesus chooses integrity, prays for wisdom, and finds unexpected provision, whether through miraculous opportunities or the inner strength to start anew.

The temptation to seek quick fixes in times of trouble is ever-present. Some turn to wealth, self-help philosophies, or distractions like entertainment and unhealthy relationships. Yet, these can only mask the emptiness for a while. Jesus offers a far deeper satisfaction when He says: *"Whoever believes in me, as Scripture has said, rivers of living water will flow from within them"* (John 7:38, NIV). Why settle for temporary relief when Jesus offers eternal nourishment? Corrie ten Boom, who survived the horrors of a concentration camp, declared, "Never be afraid to trust an unknown future to a known God." Her life stands as proof that trusting Jesus is not naïve optimism, but a wellspring of strength even in the bleakest situations.

For both present and future generations, the lesson is clear: learning to trust Jesus in uncertainty is not optional; it is essential. The world will always experience crises, shifting values, and unpredictable changes, but Christ remains the firm foundation. When personal hardship strikes or society spirals into confusion, faith in Jesus offers clarity and hope. His peace does not depend on the absence of trouble, but on the assurance of His presence. *"You will keep in perfect peace those whose minds are steadfast, because they trust in you"* (Isaiah 26:3, NIV). Just as Sarah, trembling in a hospital waiting room, discovered God's faithfulness through her husband's critical surgery, so every believer can experience this same divine peace. When all else fails, Jesus does not. The greatest legacy any generation can leave is the testimony that, in every uncertainty, trying Jesus proves He is enough.

CHAPTER TWO

THE WORLD IN THE TIME OF NOAH: A MIRROR FOR OUR GENERATION

The world during Noah's time was a place where sin reigned unchecked, and humanity drifted far from God's design. People pursued their own desires without restraint, filling the earth with violence, corruption, and immorality. This moral collapse was so severe that *"The Lord saw how great the wickedness of the human race had become on the earth, and that every inclination of the thoughts of the human heart was only evil all the time"* (Genesis 6:5, NIV). What happens to a society when it no longer seeks God's truth? History and Scripture reveal that when reverence for God is lost, chaos and destruction inevitably follow. Christian author John Piper once wrote, "Sin is what you do when your heart is not satisfied with God." This dissatisfaction with God led Noah's generation into a downward spiral a cautionary tale for every era, including our own.

In stark contrast to the world around him, Noah stood as a beacon of righteousness. His life showed that even in a corrupt generation, it is possible to live differently. *"Noah was a righteous man, blameless among the people of his time, and he walked faithfully with God"* (Genesis 6:9,

NIV). **Was Noah perfect? No, but his heart was set on honoring God rather than blending into the culture of sin.** It is often easier to follow the crowd, to compromise for acceptance but Noah chose faithfulness over popularity. Dietrich Bonhoeffer, a German pastor who resisted the evils of Nazi, said, "Being a Christian is less about cautiously avoiding sin than about courageously doing God's will." Noah courageously obeyed God, showing that faith is not just about personal survival, but about living as a witness in dark times.

When God commanded Noah to build the ark, it must have seemed outrageous. There was no visible sign of floodwaters, and the very concept of global judgment sounded absurd to those around him. Yet Noah obeyed because he trusted God's word more than human reason. *"By faith Noah, when warned about things not yet seen, in holy fear built an ark to save his family"* (Hebrews 11:7, NIV). How often do we dismiss God's guidance simply because we cannot see the outcome? Noah's story challenges us to act on faith, even when obedience seems irrational. Imagine a modern-day equivalent: someone building a massive structure in their backyard, claiming it was preparation for a divine event. Would the world not mock them just as they mocked Noah? His unwavering trust teaches that true faith is not dependent on human approval but on divine truth.

The flood itself stands as a sobering reminder of the cost of rejecting God's invitation to repentance. For decades, Noah warned his neighbors, not with words alone, but through the visible testimony of the ark under construction. Yet, the people refused to listen. *"They knew nothing about what would happen until the flood came and took them all away"* (Matthew 24:39, NIV). This is not just ancient history, it is a living warning for today's world, where many dismiss God's word as outdated, irrelevant, or inconvenient. What will it take for humanity to realize that rejecting God always leads to ruin? In his classic book Mere Christianity, C.S. Lewis wrote, "There are only two kinds of people: those who say to God, 'Thy will be done,' and those to whom God says, 'All right, then, have it your way." The people of Noah's time chose the latter, and their fate was sealed.

Yet, even in judgment, God's mercy shone brightly. The ark was not just a vessel; it was a symbol of divine grace a place of salvation offered freely to anyone willing to enter. Today, Jesus Christ is our ark, our refuge from the coming judgment upon sin. *"Salvation is found in no one else, for there is no other name under heaven given to mankind by which we must be saved"* (Acts 4:12, NIV). Just as the ark's door eventually closed, sealing the fate of those outside, one day the door of grace will also close. Will this generation choose to enter the ark of Christ's salvation or remain outside, trusting in their own strength? Noah's story teaches future generations that God's judgment is real, but His grace is greater and the wisest choice anyone can make is to trust in the refuge He provides.

NOTE THESE

1. Righteousness is possible even in a corrupt world.
2. Faith requires obedience, even when God's commands defy human logic.
3. Rejecting God's truth leads to destruction, while embracing it leads to salvation.
4. God's warnings are acts of mercy, not threats.
5. Jesus, like the ark, is the only safe place when judgment comes.

A CALL TO TRUST IN JESUS

The story of Noah is more than ancient history; it is a divine warning and a call to trust in God's way of salvation, fulfilled today through Jesus Christ. In *"When the Son of Man returns, it will be like it was in Noah's day"* (Matthew 24:37, NLT), Jesus draws a direct link between Noah's time and the world before His second coming. What made Noah's generation so dangerous was not just their immorality, but their utter disregard for God's voice. Do we not see similar patterns today, where faith is mocked, and truth is relative? Yet, in the midst of chaos, God extended grace to Noah, and today, that same grace is available to all who trust in Jesus. Philip Yancey, *What's So Amazing About Grace?* stated, *"Grace means there is nothing we can do to make God love us more, no amount of spiritual calisthenics and renunciations. And there is nothing we can do to make God love us less."* The real question is will we embrace this grace, or will we follow the crowd into destruction?

Noah's ark was more than a wooden vessel; it was a symbol of divine refuge, a place where God's mercy shielded His people from judgment. In the same way, Jesus stands as the ultimate Ark our only safe place in a world destined for divine justice. *"Yes, I am the gate. Those who come in through me will be saved"* (John 10:9, NLT). Just as Noah's family had to physically step into the ark to be saved, we must spiritually step into Christ through faith. What good would it have been if Noah admired the ark but never entered it? Today, many admire Jesus from a distance but hesitate to surrender fully. Trusting in Jesus is not about religious admiration, it's about personal surrender.

The grace God extends today is not a weak tolerance of sin, but a patient call to repentance. *"The Lord isn't really being slow about his promise, as some people think. No, he is being patient for your sake. He does not want anyone to be destroyed, but wants everyone to repent"* (2 Peter 3:9, NLT). This patience is a divine invitation, a window of mercy. But windows eventually close. How long will humanity mock God's call before judgment falls? Consider the days before the flood, life carried on as usual until the rain began to fall. Likewise, today, people marry, work, and pursue dreams with no thought of God. Yet, just as the flood came suddenly, so will the return of Christ. Christian author Leonard Ravenhill warned, "The opportunity of a lifetime must be seized within the lifetime of the opportunity."

The life of C.S. Lewis offers a powerful example of how grace can reach even the most skeptical heart. Once an atheist, Lewis fiercely resisted the claims of Christ, yet God patiently pursued him. Through the gentle influence of Christian friends and deep personal reflection, Lewis came to see that the Gospel was not a myth but the ultimate truth. In his book *Surprised by Joy*, Lewis describes his conversion as being "brought in, kicking, struggling, resentful, and darting his eyes in every direction for a chance of escape." Yet that reluctant step of trust led him into a life of profound purpose, influencing millions through his writings. Is there anyone today too skeptical or too hardened for God's grace to reach? Lewis's life answers: absolutely not.

The story of Saul, who became Paul, reinforces this truth: no one is beyond God's reach. *"Saul was uttering threats with every breath and was eager to kill the Lord's followers"* (Acts 9:1, NLT). Yet, on the road to Damascus, grace knocked him off his horse and opened his eyes to a new reality. From persecutor to preacher, his life became a living testimony of God's power to transform. What if Ananias had refused to go to Saul, thinking him too dangerous to approach? What if Saul had hardened his heart? Thankfully, God's grace triumphed, and Saul became Paul, a reminder that divine purpose often begins at the end of human pride. This teaches future generations that no failure, no sin, and no rebellion is greater than God's power to redeem. Whether you are a skeptic like Lewis, or a rebel like Saul, the call to trust in Jesus stands open. The ark is ready, the question is, will you enter before the rain begins to fall?

THE SILENCE OF GOD AND PERSONAL SALVATION

The story of Noah is rich with lessons about faith, obedience, and divine judgment, but one curious silence stands out, the Bible does not explicitly describe the personal faith of Noah's wife and children. While Noah's righteousness is highlighted, the spiritual condition of his family is left unspoken. This silence raises a critical question: Did God save his family because of their individual faith, or were they spared because of Noah's obedience? *"Noah was a righteous man, the only blameless person living on earth at the time, and he walked in close fellowship with God"*

(Genesis 6:9, NLT). This verse highlights Noah's personal relationship with God, but says nothing of his family's own commitment. Could this omission be intentional to emphasize that salvation is ultimately personal, requiring each soul to respond individually to God's call?

Ezekiel 14:14 reinforces this truth: *"Even if Noah, Daniel, and Job were there, their righteousness would save no one but themselves, says the Sovereign Lord"* (NLT). This scripture directly dismantles the notion that faith can be inherited or transferred. Noah's faith positioned his family to witness God's work firsthand, but it could not save them without their own response. This is a sobering reminder for families today while parents, pastors, and mentors can point the way, they cannot walk the path for anyone else. Charles Spurgeon wrote, *"You cannot have Christ's blessings without Christ Himself." Each generation must decide anew whether they will follow Christ or reject Him. Can anyone be saved simply because they were raised in a Christian home or regularly attended church? Scripture answers with a resounding "No."*

This truth is vividly illustrated in countless real-life stories, like that of a faithful mother who prays daily for her daughter who has strayed from the faith. Despite the mother's godly life, the daughter chooses a path of rebellion, believing her mother's prayers will somehow cover her. Yet it is only after the daughter faces a personal crisis, a broken relationship, and deep depression that she realizes her need for her own relationship with Jesus. In tears, she prays, not because her mother wants her to, but because she desires to know the Savior herself. *"For everyone who calls on the name of the Lord will be saved"* (Romans 10:13, NLT). This testimony reflects the very heart of salvation: personal surrender.

The silence in Noah's story also teaches us that God values personal faith over religious inheritance. The ark was a physical refuge, but each member of Noah's family had to choose to step inside. No one was dragged in against their will. Likewise, Jesus offers Himself as the door to salvation, but each heart must choose to walk through. *"I am the gate; those who come in through me will be saved"* (John 10:9, NLT). No spouse, parent, or friend can make that choice for another.

As Oswald Chambers wrote, "We are not asked to believe the Bible, but to believe the One whom the Bible reveals." The ark stands ready, but the decision belongs to each individual.

For future generations, the lesson is clear: personal faith matters. The prayers of faithful ancestors lay a foundation, but they do not replace the need for personal repentance and commitment. Just as Noah's family had to walk into the ark themselves, each person must step into Christ's saving grace. This truth challenges cultural Christianity, where identity is often based on family tradition rather than personal conviction. The silence about Noah's family's faith is not an oversight it is a divine reminder that no one can hide behind someone else's righteousness. The ultimate question echoes through the ages: Have you made your own decision to enter the ark of salvation, or are you simply standing near it, hoping someone else's faith will carry you through?

THE INDIVIDUAL NATURE OF FAITH

Faith is ultimately a personal decision that no one can make on behalf of another. From the very beginning, God has extended His invitation to humanity, yet He never forces anyone into fellowship with Him. This truth is vividly illustrated in Noah's story, where Noah's faith is highlighted, but the Bible leaves room for speculation about the personal faith of his family. Noah believed God's warning about the flood, obeyed His command to build the ark, and through that obedience, secured salvation for himself and his household. However, *"It was by faith that Noah built a large boat to save his family from the flood. He obeyed God, who warned him about things that had never happened before"* (Hebrews 11:7, NLT). This shows that while Noah's faith opened a door for his family, each of them had to decide whether to trust Noah's message and enter the ark themselves. This illustrates a critical truth for today's believers: faith cannot be secondhand; it must be personal.

This personal nature of faith is further emphasized by Paul's words in *Romans 10:9: "If you openly declare that Jesus is Lord and believe in your heart that God raised him from the dead, you will be saved"* (NLT). Notice the emphasis on personal confession and belief. No parent, pastor, or spiritual mentor can do this for another person. Faith is not inherited like family wealth or passed on like a family name. Charles Spurgeon affirmed, "A man is not saved because his mother was a saint. Grace does not run in the blood." This underscores that while godly influence matters, personal response is what counts for salvation. How many today are relying on their family's faith, believing that being born into a Christian home secures their eternal destiny?

The Bible also reminds us that individual faith is the basis for divine judgment and reward. *"For the Son of Man will come with His angels in the glory of His Father and will judge all people according to their deeds"* (Matthew 16:27, NLT). This verse highlights the personal accountability that comes with faith. Noah's family walked into the ark themselves; they were not carried in against their will. In the same way, attending church or participating in religious activities will never replace the need for personal surrender to Christ. Dietrich Bonhoeffer, the great theologian, wrote, "The call to follow Jesus is a personal call. It is addressed to you and me individually." This personal calling means that every person must ask themselves: Have I truly tried Jesus for myself, or am I just walking in the shadow of others' faith?

This principle is not just a biblical theory but is seen in everyday life. Take the story of a successful businessman who was raised in a Christian home. His parents prayed daily and served faithfully in the church. Yet, as the man grew older, he drifted from faith, believing his family's devotion was enough. After a serious health scare, he was forced to confront the fragility of life and realized that his parents' faith could not save him. Alone in a hospital room, he prayed and personally surrendered to Jesus. *"Come close to God, and God will come close to you"* (James 4:8, NLT). This moment marked the beginning of his own journey of faith, a choice only he could make.

For current and future generations, the lesson is clear: salvation is personal, not communal. Just as Noah's family had to walk into the ark themselves, every individual today must choose to enter the "ark" of

Jesus Christ. Parents and mentors can guide and pray, but they cannot believe for their children. This truth challenges cultural Christianity, where people often rely on family traditions or church attendance instead of genuine faith. As the world grows more uncertain, this question becomes even more urgent: *Have you personally tried Jesus?* The ark of grace stands open, but only those who choose to enter will find eternal safety.

NOTE THESE

1. Salvation is a personal decision that no one else can make for you.

2. Faith cannot be inherited from parents, family, or community it must come from your own heart.

3. Being part of a religious group or attending church does not guarantee salvation without personal belief in Jesus.

4. God's invitation to salvation is open to all, but only those who choose to respond will receive it.

5. Every generation must personally decide to trust in Jesus, as faith is not passed down automatically.

THE FAMILY SAVED BY FAITH

The story of Noah and his family stands as a remarkable testament to the power of faith in a world overcome by evil. Out of millions, only eight individuals found salvation not because they were the largest or the strongest, but because they trusted God when no one else would. **Noah's faith set him apart, and it created a path for his family to follow, demonstrating how obedience to God can influence those closest to us.** Yet, this story also sparks deep reflection: Did Noah's family enter the ark solely because of his faith, or did they develop their own personal trust in God's plan? *"It was by faith that Noah built a large boat to save his family from the flood. He obeyed God, who warned him about things that had never happened before. By his faith Noah condemned the rest of the world, and he received the righteousness that comes by faith."* (Hebrews 11:7,

NLT). This scripture highlights that Noah's faith was the foundation of his family's salvation, but it does not directly reveal their individual beliefs, leaving room for multiple perspectives.

One view emphasizes Noah's faith as the primary covering that saved his household, a reflection of spiritual leadership within families. Just as Abraham's faith paved the way for his descendants to walk in covenant with God, so Noah's obedience opened the door of salvation for his family. However, another perspective argues that each member had to exercise their own measure of faith by stepping into the ark. No one was physically forced inside; they could have refused. *"If you openly declare that Jesus is Lord and believe in your heart that God raised him from the dead, you will be saved."* (Romans 10:9, NLT). This verse highlights that salvation comes through personal confession and belief, reinforcing the idea that Noah's family members had to personally choose to trust God's plan. John Stott, Basic Christianity, wrote, "Faith is a reasoning trust, a trust which reckons thoughtfully and confidently upon the trustworthiness of God."

The silence of Scripture regarding the individual faith journeys of Noah's wife, sons, and daughters-in-law leaves space for speculation, but it also highlights an important truth for every generation: faith cannot be inherited. This lesson applies strongly today, where many assume they are saved because they were raised in Christian homes or attend church regularly. Yet, *"For the Son of Man will come with his angels in the glory of his Father and will judge all people according to their deeds."* (Matthew 16:27, NLT). Personal faith and action, not family history determine eternal destiny. Leonard Ravenhill stated, "God doesn't have favorites, but He does have intimates, and they are the ones who seek Him." This quote reminds us that intimacy with God is not inherited or assumed, it is personally pursued and individually embraced.

Practical examples make this truth even clearer. Imagine a family where the father is a pastor, faithfully preaching the gospel every Sunday. His children, however, must still make their own decision to follow Christ. One child may embrace the faith, while another may walk away despite hearing the same sermons. The ark represents Christ, a shelter from judgment, but no one can be carried into it by someone else's faith. *"For God loved the world so much that he gave his one and only Son, so that everyone who believes in him will not perish but have eternal life."* (John 3:16, NLT). This offer is extended to all, but it demands a personal response from each heart.

Ultimately, Noah's story teaches that faith requires both belief and action. Noah believed God, but his belief moved him to build the ark and prepare for the flood. His family's decision to enter that ark demonstrated their own faith in God's word, even though the full extent of their personal belief is left unspoken in Scripture. This silence challenges each generation to examine their own response to God's call. Will we choose to enter the ark of salvation through faith in Jesus, or will we remain outside, consumed by the world's distractions? The door stands open today, but just as in Noah's time, it will not remain open forever. Trying Jesus is not just a religious option; it is the only pathway to eternal safety and peace.

SALVATION THROUGH OBEDIENCE AND FAITH

The story of Noah and his family offers a profound lesson about salvation, showing that obedience and faith are inseparable when walking with God. In a world where the majority lived in wickedness, Noah stood apart because he obeyed God's instructions and built the ark. His faith and obedience were not based on what made sense to society, but on trusting God's word. This challenges us to ask: Do we follow God even when His commands go against cultural norms? *"You can enter God's Kingdom only through the narrow gate. The highway to hell is broad, and its gate is wide for the many who choose that way."* (Matthew 7:13, NLT). Jesus' words confirm that true salvation has never been about blending into the majority; it is about choosing a path that requires both personal faith and obedience to God's revealed truth.

There are different views on how obedience and faith work together in salvation. Some believe that faith alone saves, citing, *"God saved you by his grace when you believed. And you can't take credit for this; it is a gift from God."* (Ephesians 2:8, NLT). This emphasizes that salvation is not earned but received through belief in Christ. Others, however, stress that true faith must produce obedience. As James famously wrote, "Just as the body is dead without breath, so also faith is dead without good works." (James 2:26, NLT). Noah's obedience was evidence of his faith. He believed God's warning about the flood, but that belief led him to act he built the ark. This raises a critical question for today: Can someone truly have faith if their life shows no evidence of obedience?

Noah's family's salvation also illustrates the connection between individual and household faith. Noah's personal obedience set an example for his household, but each family member had to decide to enter the ark themselves. This mirrors how salvation through Jesus works today. *"They replied, 'Believe in the Lord Jesus and you will be saved, along with everyone in your household.'"* (Acts 16:31, NLT). However, this promise does not imply automatic salvation for family members; rather, it highlights how a believer's faith can influence others to follow Christ. Elisabeth Elliot said, "Faith does not eliminate questions. But faith knows where to take them." Noah's faith influenced his family to trust God enough to follow him into the ark, but their personal decision to step inside was their own act of faith.

This principle holds a critical lesson for current and future generations. In a world saturated with social pressures, opinions, and trends, it is tempting to assume safety lies in the majority's approval. However, salvation has never been about popularity. It is about choosing obedience to God's word, even when it means standing alone. This applies practically in today's world, where students, professionals, and families often face pressure to conform to cultural or moral compromises. A Christian student standing firm in biblical truth on a secular campus mirrors Noah building the ark in a corrupt generation. *"If you openly declare that Jesus is Lord and believe in your heart that God raised him from the dead, you will be saved."* (Romans 10:9, NLT). Declaring faith in Jesus often requires the courage to stand against popular opinion.

Finally, Noah's story teaches that true salvation requires more than just intellectual belief it calls for obedient action rooted in trust. Just as Noah did not only believe God's warning but also built the ark, we are called not just to believe in Jesus but to follow His teachings daily. This obedience, even when difficult, is the evidence of authentic faith. Renowned evangelist Billy Graham once said, "Faith is taking the first step even when you don't see the whole staircase." Trying Jesus means walking that narrow path obeying God's word even when the world mocks it, trusting His promises even when they seem distant, and choosing eternal life over temporary comfort. This is the call to every generation: Will you walk by faith and obey, or will you follow the crowd to destruction?

A WORLD IN DARKNESS: THE NEED FOR SPIRITUAL AWAKENING

The Bible warns that a time will come when spiritual darkness will cover the earth, leading many to reject truth and embrace wickedness. This is not merely a lack of physical light but a state of deep moral and spiritual blindness. *"Darkness as black as night covers all the nations of the earth, but the glory of the Lord rises and appears over you."* (Isaiah 60:2, NLT). Today, we see evidence of this prophecy unfolding moral values are declining, truth is being replaced by deception, and people prioritize self-gratification over spiritual wisdom. Society often promotes materialism, pleasure, and success as the highest goals, while biblical principles are dismissed as outdated or restrictive. But does rejecting God's truth truly bring freedom, or does it lead to further bondage? C.S. Lewis wrote, "If you look for truth, you may find comfort in the end; if you look for comfort, you will get neither truth nor comfort." Seeking temporary comfort in sin only deepens the darkness, while pursuing God's truth leads to real freedom and light.

Jesus warned that before His return, the world would resemble the days of Noah, a time marked by widespread corruption and indifference to God. *"When the Son of Man returns, it will be like it was in Noah's day."*

(Matthew 24:37, NLT). This description is strikingly relevant today, as violence, immorality, and moral relativism dominate global culture. Many choose to live as if there are no consequences for sin, ignoring the call to repentance. Yet, even in the midst of this spiritual decay, God calls His people to stand firm. Paul urged believers to seize every opportunity for righteousness, knowing that the world's condition is deteriorating: *"Make the most of every opportunity in these evil days."* (Ephesians 5:16, NLT). This is a call to reject compromise, to be vigilant in faith, and to shine as lights in a world that increasingly prefers darkness over truth. But are we willing to live differently when it means standing against the current of culture?

History offers powerful examples of transformation from darkness to light, one of the most notable being John Newton. Once a ruthless slave trader, Newton lived a life of selfishness and sin, profiting from human suffering. However, during a terrifying storm at sea, he cried out to God for mercy, marking the beginning of his spiritual awakening. Over time, he repented, abandoned his wicked past, and became a leading advocate for the abolition of slavery. His most famous hymn, *Amazing Grace*, reflects the depth of his transformation: "I once was lost, but now am found; was blind, but now I see." This story reminds us that no one is beyond God's reach. His grace is sufficient to redeem even the most broken souls. How often do we judge others as being too far gone, forgetting that God's light can penetrate even the darkest hearts?

Ultimately, every person must decide whether to remain in darkness or step into the light of Christ. Spiritual blindness is dangerous because it deceives people into thinking they are fine while leading them further from God. Yet, God's invitation to salvation remains open. *"For once you were full of darkness, but now you have light from the Lord. So live as people of light!"* (Ephesians 5:8, NLT). Walking in the light means choosing Christ over sin, truth over deception, and righteousness over worldly compromise. In today's world, where moral confusion reigns, will we be bold enough to follow Jesus, or will we be swept away by the growing darkness? The decision we make today will shape not only our own lives but also the generations that come after us.

NOTE THESE

1. Spiritual darkness increases when people reject God's truth and embrace sin, but God's light is always available for those who seek Him.//
2. The world's moral decline is a sign that believers must stand firm in faith and live as lights in the darkness.
3. No one is too lost for God's grace, and true repentance can transform even the most sinful life.
4. Personal choices to follow or reject God have eternal consequences for individuals and future generations.
5. Choosing to walk in God's light brings purpose, hope, and the promise of eternal life.

3

CHAPTER THREE

LIGHT IN THE DARKNESS

The imagery of a man wandering through a dark forest without light paints a vivid picture of the human condition without Christ. Darkness represents confusion, sin, fear, and separation from God. In contrast, Jesus offers Himself as the guiding light that leads us out of spiritual confusion and into divine truth. *Jesus spoke to the people once more and said, "I am the light of the world. If you follow me, you won't have to walk in darkness, because you will have the light that leads to life."* (John 8:12, NLT). This statement is profound. Jesus does not simply show the way; He *is* the way. Yet, do we not live-in times when many reject this light, preferring the temporary thrills of darkness? **When Jesus becomes our light, our entire worldview shifts, and we begin to see life, purpose, and eternity through the lens of truth.**

The role of believers is not only to follow the light but to *be* light in the world. Jesus reminds us in *Matthew 5:14-16 (NLT): "You are the light of the world like a city on a hilltop that cannot be hidden... let your good deeds shine out for all to see, so that everyone will praise your heavenly Father."* This means our actions, attitudes, and values should reflect Christ, illuminating the path for others. In a generation where corruption, immorality, and compromise often prevail, will the world see the light of Jesus shining through His people? Dietrich Bonhoeffer wrote, "Your life as a Christian should make non-believers question their disbelief in God." If Christians blend into the darkness around them, how will they fulfill their calling as light-bearers? This challenges believers today to stand firm in faith, love, and truth becoming moral and spiritual compasses for society.

In practical terms, this call to shine can be seen in everyday decisions; how we treat others, how we respond to injustice, how we handle crises, and how we prioritize our lives. Imagine a student who refuses to cheat during exams because of their Christian convictions, even when peers mock them. Or a businessperson who chooses honesty over profit, trusting that God honors integrity. These are real-life ways the light of Christ pierces through darkness. *Your word is a lamp to guide my feet and a light for my path.* (Psalm 119:105, NLT). The Word of God becomes both the source and the fuel for that light, shaping decisions and guiding steps. Without this divine light, even the most intelligent minds stumble in spiritual blindness.

Ultimately, Jesus offers a simple yet life-changing invitation: *"I am the way, the truth, and the life. No one can come to the Father except through me."* (John 14:6, NLT). This truth cuts through all cultural confusion and religious alternatives. It reminds future generations that light and darkness cannot coexist they must choose one. Will they walk in the blinding distractions of sin, or will they step into the brilliance of God's grace? For current and future believers, the lesson is clear: the world's darkness will only intensify, but the light of Christ will always shine brighter for those willing to follow it. The choice is personal, urgent, and eternal.

THE REALITY OF HARDSHIP

The reality of hardship is an undeniable truth that both scripture and life experience affirm. Many people cling to the hope that things will eventually get better, that the economy will stabilize, conflicts will end, and peace will reign. However, the Bible paints a different picture. *"You should know this, Timothy, that in the last days there will be very difficult times."* (2 Timothy 3:1, NLT). Hardship is not an interruption to life it is part of life's journey, especially for those who follow Christ. Does this mean God has abandoned the world? Not at all. Instead, He uses hardship to awaken hearts, draw people closer to Him, and refine faith like gold through fire. As the beloved

One clear example of hardship today is economic instability. Prices continue to rise while incomes stagnate, leaving families struggling to afford even the basics. Imagine a mother going to the market with a budget she has carefully planned, only to find that the food prices have doubled overnight. This scenario is no longer uncommon but reflects a global trend of economic hardship. Jesus Himself warned us that *"Here on earth you will have many trials and sorrows. But take heart, because I have overcome the world."* (John 16:33, NLT). The reality of hardship is not a sign that God has lost control, but a reminder that this world is temporary and flawed; our ultimate hope must rest in Christ.

Different views arise when people face hardships. Some see difficulties as punishment from God, while others recognize them as opportunities for growth and deeper dependence on Him. A man who lost his job, home, and savings could easily fall into despair, blaming God for his misfortune. But when he turned to Jesus in his brokenness, he found peace that surpassed understanding. *"And this same God who takes care of me will supply all your needs from His glorious riches, which have been given to us in Christ Jesus."* (Philippians 4:19, NLT). The job offer that came after months of rejection wasn't glamorous, but it was God's provision, reminding him that divine help often comes in unexpected forms. Is it not true that many times, God's provision comes disguised as humble opportunities?

Christian thinkers like Charles Spurgeon have long emphasized that trials are God's tools for shaping character. Spurgeon once said, "The Lord gets his best soldiers out of the highlands of affliction." The storms of life teach lessons that ease and comfort never could. For future generations, this lesson is crucial: hardship will come, but God's faithfulness will always outlast the storm. Psalm 34:19 (NLT) declares, *"The righteous person faces many troubles, but the Lord comes to the rescue each time."* This is not a promise to remove all trials but to walk with us through them. Whether it's financial struggles, health crises, or personal loss, God's presence sustains us when we surrender to His will.

The call to trust Jesus in times of hardship is not just a religious cliché but a lifeline for every generation. The storms of today may differ from those of the past, but the anchor remains the same, Jesus Christ. What will future generations do when life turns upside down? Will they cling to fleeting solutions, or will they turn to the eternal Rock of Ages? This is the ultimate lesson: hardship will come, but God will remain faithful, and those who anchor their hope in Christ will find strength, peace, and purpose even in life's darkest moments.

FIND STRENGTH AND PEACE IN JESUS

In a world filled with uncertainty and turmoil, the call to find strength and peace in Jesus is more relevant than ever. When Jesus said, *"Don't let your hearts be troubled. Trust in God and also trust in me."* (John 14:1, NLT), He was not speaking to people living in comfort but to disciples about to face persecution or loss and fear. This reveals an important truth: the peace Jesus offers is not dependent on circumstances it is rooted in God's unchanging nature. Just as God preserved Noah in the midst of a world facing destruction, those who trust in Jesus today are sustained by His divine protection. *"God is our refuge and strength, always ready to help in times of trouble."* (Psalm 46:1, NLT). If peace is not found in Jesus, where else can it be found? Is it in wealth, which can vanish overnight? Or in human relationships, which are often fragile?

The story of a woman who lost her job unexpectedly highlights the practical reality of trusting God in the face of hardship. With bills mounting and no clear path forward, fear and anxiety threatened to overwhelm her. Yet, rather than allowing despair to consume her, she turned to Jesus and held tightly to His promise: *"Don't worry about anything; instead, pray about everything. Tell God what you need, and thank him for all he has done. Then you will experience God's peace, which exceeds anything we can understand."* (Philippians 4:6-7, NLT). Through prayer and thanksgiving, her heart found peace, and God provided through an unexpected connection. Isn't this how God often works—opening doors we never saw coming? Her testimony reminds us that even when all seems lost, Jesus remains our provider and peace-giver.

Different views exist when it comes to handling adversity. Some believe that peace comes from controlling every detail of life—building wealth, planning for every emergency, and relying on human systems. Others, however, realize that true peace comes only from surrendering to Jesus, the Prince of Peace. Christian author Andrew Murray once wrote, *"God is ready to assume full responsibility for the life wholly yielded to Him."* This is the heart of Christian peace, not avoiding hardship but trusting that God walks with us through it. *"You will keep in perfect peace all who trust in you, all whose thoughts are fixed on you!"* (Isaiah 26:3, NLT). This is a peace that does not crumble when storms hit because its foundation is Christ Himself.

For current and future generations, this lesson is critical. Technology may advance, economies may shift, and political landscapes may change, but one truth will remain: life's storms will come. **The question is not if hardships will arise, but where we will anchor our faith when they do. Will we cling to temporary comforts or place our hope in the eternal rock, Jesus Christ?** This is the wisdom that must be passed down to seek peace not in the absence of trouble but in the presence of Christ.

In the end, the story of Noah, the testimony of the woman who lost her job, and the timeless promises of scripture all point to the same reality: Jesus is our only lasting source of peace and strength. His peace does not make sense to the world because it surpasses understanding. But for those who choose to trust Him, this peace becomes a shield for the heart and mind. When future storms arise, will we surely panic, or will we, like Noah, build an ark of faith and trust God for the outcome?

That is the challenge for every generation to find strength and peace not in the world but in Jesus alone.

EMBRACE THE END WITH JESUS

The story of Noah and the ark offers a sobering picture of God's grace and judgment. For years, Noah preached and warned the people about the coming flood, but they ignored him. Finally, the day came when *"the Lord closed the door behind them."* (Genesis 7:16, NLT). This moment highlights an eternal truth: God's grace has a time limit. He patiently calls people to repentance, but when the appointed time arrives, the door to salvation closes. **Just as in Noah's time, today's world is being warned of a coming end, an end where Jesus will return to judge the living and the dead.** Yet, in His mercy, God still extends an invitation for all to enter the "ark" of salvation through Christ. Why do so many ignore this invitation, assuming they have endless time?

Jesus Himself echoed this urgent call when He said, *"Anyone who is thirsty may come to me! Anyone who believes in me may come and drink!"* (John 7:37-38, NLT). This open invitation is a symbol of both grace and urgency. The living water Jesus offers is not just a temporary relief, but a source of eternal life. Yet, many delay their response, assuming they can accept His offer later, perhaps when life slows down or when they face a crisis. **But does tomorrow belong to anyone?** *"For God says, 'At just the right time, I heard you. On the day of salvation, I helped you.' Indeed, the 'right time' is now. Today is the day of salvation."* (2 Corinthians 6:2, NLT). This shows that waiting is a dangerous gamble, for the door may close at any moment.

Consider the story of David, a man consumed by career success and worldly pleasures. He knew about Jesus but believed there was plenty of time to surrender his life. His health crisis became a wake-up call, forcing him to confront the reality of life's fragility. In that hospital bed, David remembered the invitation of Christ: *"But those who drink the water I give will never be thirsty again. It becomes a fresh, bubbling spring within them, giving them eternal life."* (John 4:14, NLT). Faced with mortality, he realized that wealth and success could not save him. He prayed for salvation, and though his health improved, it was the peace of knowing Jesus that truly transformed him. Isn't this a lesson for all of us that life's comforts are fleeting, but the peace of Christ is eternal?

Some view God's judgment as harsh or unloving, but this is a limited understanding of divine justice. God is both loving and just, offering grace for a season and accountability at the appointed time. Renowned preacher David Platt wrote, "Every saved person this side of heaven owes the gospel to every lost person this side of hell." This highlights the urgency of the gospel; Christians are called not only to accept the invitation for themselves but to passionately share it with others. *"Work hard to show the results of your salvation, obeying God with deep reverence and fear."* (Philippians 2:12, NLT). True love warns others when danger is near, just as Noah warned his generation. Are we warning ours?

For both current and future generations, this message carries profound lessons. The world promotes self-sufficiency, success, and personal comfort as the ultimate goals, but Scripture teaches us that life is fragile and temporary. The door to grace is open now, but it will not remain so forever. *"Look, I am coming soon, bringing my reward with me to repay all people according to their deeds."* (Revelation 22:12, NLT). Tomorrow is never promised, and delaying a response to Jesus is a risk no one can afford to take. For those who embrace Jesus now, there is not only the assurance of eternal life, but also the peace of knowing that even in uncertain times, they are safe in the ark of God's grace. Will we, like Noah, prepare for what is to come, or will we, like the crowds outside the ark, dismiss the warnings until it's too late?

JESUS, GOD'S REDEMPTION AND THE PATH TO NEW BEGINNINGS

When sin first entered the world through Adam and Eve's disobedience, humanity became separated from God, unable to bridge the gap through human effort alone. But even in that moment of separation, God had a plan for redemption, a plan that would one day be fulfilled through Jesus Christ. Jesus became the bridge, the way back to a restored relationship with the Father. As Jesus Himself declared, *"Anyone who is thirsty may come to me! Anyone who believes in me may come and drink! For the Scriptures declare, 'Rivers of living water will flow from his heart.'"* (John 7:37-38, NLT). This invitation wasn't just about meeting spiritual thirst temporarily, but about offering a new beginning a chance for humanity to walk with God once again. Can anything in this world truly satisfy the soul apart from God? History and personal experience reveal that worldly pursuits leave people empty, but Jesus offers living water that satisfies eternally.

In the Old Testament, God's Spirit would rest on select individuals for specific purposes, prophets, priests, and kings, but this access to God's presence was limited. Through Jesus, that access was permanently opened. The promise of John 7:38 came to life at Pentecost when the Holy Spirit was poured out upon all believers, not just the spiritual elite. This transformation isn't just external; it is internal and lasting. *"This means that anyone who belongs to Christ has become a new person. The old life is gone; a new life has begun!"* (2 Corinthians 5:17, NLT). What could be more hopeful than knowing that no matter how broken, sinful, or lost someone feels, Jesus offers a fresh start? Max Lucado said, "God loves you just the way you are, but He refuses to leave you that way. He wants you to be just like Jesus." This is the power of redemption not just being saved from sin, but being transformed into someone who reflects Christ.

The living water Jesus speaks of is the Holy Spirit, and He doesn't just cleanse; He empowers. When a person accepts Christ, they don't only receive forgiveness they receive God Himself living within them. This divine presence equips them to walk in righteousness, love, and boldness, even in a hostile world. *"For God is working in you, giving you the desire and the power to do what pleases him."* (Philippians 2:13,

NLT). This is not self-improvement but Spirit-empowerment. For example, Corrie ten Boom, a woman who endured the horrors of a Nazi concentration camp during World War II. She lost family members, suffered immense trauma, and battled with the pain of forgiveness. Yet, when she surrendered her heart fully to Christ, the Holy Spirit gave her the strength to forgive her captors and the courage to travel the world, sharing her testimony of hope and healing. Is this not a powerful picture of how Jesus not only redeems but empowers His people to walk in the newness of life?

This invitation to new beginnings is not limited to a select few it is for everyone. Jesus doesn't call only the righteous or those with religious backgrounds; He calls the broken, the weary, and the rejected. *"Then Jesus said, 'Come to me, all of you who are weary and carry heavy burdens, and I will give you rest.'"* (Matthew 11:28, NLT). It doesn't matter how far someone has wandered, how deeply they've sinned, or how hopeless they feel. Jesus' arms are open wide, offering forgiveness, restoration, and a completely new identity. As Tim Keller wrote, "Jesus Christ did not come to earth to bring judgment. He came to bear it." This truth should shake Christians out of complacency and stir a sense of urgency to share this hope with others.

For both present and future generations, the lesson is clear: true life and purpose begin with Jesus. In a world obsessed with self-sufficiency and personal achievement, Jesus offers something radically different: a life anchored in His unchanging love, empowered by His Spirit, and directed by His perfect plan. *"My purpose is to give them a rich and satisfying life."* (John 10:10, NLT). This is not a life free from struggles but a life where those struggles are faced with divine strength and eternal hope. Will future generations chase temporary pleasures, or will they drink deeply from the living water that only Christ can give? The path to new beginnings is open to all who are willing to follow Jesus, the One who redeems, restores, and renews.

NOTE THESE

1. Jesus is the only bridge that restores our broken relationship with God.
2. True transformation comes not from human effort but through the indwelling power of the Holy Spirit.
3. No one is too lost or broken for Jesus to redeem and offer a fresh start.
4. The invitation to come to Jesus is open to everyone, regardless of their past.
5. Life's fullest meaning and lasting peace can only be found in Jesus Christ.

CHAPTER FOUR

THE REALITY OF SPIRITUAL BATTLES

Spiritual battles are a reality that every Christian must face, whether they are aware of it or not. The Bible makes it clear that life is not only about what we see with our physical eyes, but also about unseen forces at work in the spiritual realm. In *Ephesians 6:12 (NIV)*, Paul reminds us: *"For our struggle is not against flesh and blood, but against the rulers, against the authorities, against the powers of this dark world and against the spiritual forces of evil in the heavenly realms."* This means that many of the challenges we encounter, fear, doubt, temptation, and discouragement are not just natural occurrences but manifestations of spiritual warfare. Some may argue that life's difficulties are purely psychological or environmental, but the Bible teaches that believers are caught in a greater cosmic conflict between good and evil. As Francis Schaeffer wrote in *Mere Christianity*, *"There is no place in this universe where we can say, 'This is neutral ground.' All of life is spiritual, and every decision counts."* This calls for spiritual alertness and preparation, knowing that our faith will be tested.

In spiritual battles, believers must recognize that the enemy's primary goal is to weaken our faith, distort God's truth, and separate us from the peace found in Christ. However, God has not left us defenseless. *2 Corinthians 10:4 (NIV)* declares: *"The weapons we fight with are not the weapons of the world. On the contrary, they have divine power to demolish stronghold."* This reveals that through prayer, the Word of God, and the power of the Holy Spirit, we have all we need to overcome the enemy's schemes. Yet, some Christians underestimate these battles, thinking that attending church or doing good deeds is enough to shield them. But spiritual warfare is fought daily in the mind, heart, and spirit. Renowned author Dallas Willard once said, *"The greatest danger to the Christian church today is that of being conformed to the world rather than being transformed by Christ."* This quote challenges us to reflect on the internal compromises we often make, where the real enemy may be the subtle shaping of our hearts and minds by worldly desires rather than outward persecution. The lesson for today's generation is clear: spiritual complacency is dangerous, and believers must be intentional about cultivating a strong and vigilant faith life.

A practical example is the story of a young man who struggled with addiction. Every time he tried to break free, he felt an unseen pull dragging him back. No amount of willpower alone could give him lasting victory. It was only when he surrendered fully to Christ, engaged in prayer, and filled his mind with Scripture that he began to experience freedom. His story reminds us of *James 4:7 (NIV)*: *"Submit yourselves, then, to God. Resist the devil, and he will flee from you."* Spiritual battles are real, but God's power is greater. For future generations, the message is this: Do not neglect the reality of spiritual warfare. Equip yourself daily with God's truth, stand firm in faith, and remember that victory is assured for those who trust in Christ. John Piper rightly said, "The only possible attitude toward outbursts of evil in the world is to fight." Christians are called not only to believe, but to fight the good fight of faith, knowing that ultimate victory belongs to the Lord.

VICTORY THROUGH CHRIST IN SPIRITUAL BATTLES

Spiritual battles are an unavoidable reality in the life of every believer. Although, many people focus solely on the visible challenges of life, finances, relationships and careers. Scripture reveals that there is a far greater, invisible war being waged. The enemy, Satan, actively works to plant seeds of doubt, fear, and temptation in the hearts of believers, attempting to separate them from God's truth. *1 Peter 5:8 (NIV)* warns us: *"Be alert and of sober mind. Your enemy the devil prowls around like a roaring lion looking for someone to devour."* This reminder calls us to spiritual vigilance because ignoring the reality of these battles does not make them disappear. John MacArthur affirmed, *"Satan is most effective in the church when he comes not as an open enemy, but as a false friend; not when he persecutes the church, but when he joins it; not when he attacks the pulpit, but when he stands in it."* If the enemy knows the power believers possess, should we not be equally aware and prepared to stand firm?

One of the greatest deceptions the enemy uses is to convince people that spiritual battles do not exist. In today's world, many view life's struggles through the lens of psychology, sociology, or personal failure, ignoring the spiritual forces behind these challenges. However, the Bible makes it clear in *Ephesians 6:12 (NIV)*: *"For our struggle is not against flesh and blood, but against the rulers, against the authorities, against the powers of this dark world and against the spiritual forces of evil in the heavenly realms."* This spiritual war is fought not with physical weapons but with faith, prayer, and the Word of God. C.S. Lewis highlighted this truth in The Screwtape Letters, writing: "There are two equal and opposite errors into which our race can fall about the devils: one is to disbelieve in their existence, and the other is to feel an excessive and unhealthy interest in them." Believers must strike the balance and acknowledge the battle without living in fear, knowing that Christ has already secured the ultimate victory.

The promise of victory through Christ is not an abstract concept; it is a living reality for those who trust and follow Him. *John 16:33 (NIV)* declares: *"I have told you these things, so that in me you may have peace. In this world, you will have trouble. But take heart! I have overcome the world."* This assurance does not mean believers will avoid hardship; instead, it means they can face every spiritual attack with confidence, knowing they are not alone. Consider the practical example of a woman called into ministry who faced overwhelming fear and doubt whenever she tried to step forward. Each time she prepared to speak God's Word, she battled anxiety and discouragement. However, through prayer, fasting, and encouragement from fellow believers, she overcame these attacks and boldly fulfilled her calling. Her story demonstrates that victory is not achieved by human strength alone, but through reliance on God's power.

For current and future generations, the lessons are clear: spiritual complacency is dangerous, and ignoring spiritual warfare leaves believers vulnerable to the enemy's schemes. Prayer, the Word of God, and fellowship with other believers are essential tools for victory. As *Ephesians 6:11 (NIV)* instructs: *"Put on the full armor of God, so that you can take your stand against the devil's schemes."* This armor is not optional; it is essential for survival in spiritual battles. Believers must also remember that victory is not just for personal benefit. When we stand firm, we inspire others to trust God and fight their own battles with faith. Billy Graham said, "Courage is contagious. When a brave man takes a stand, the spines of others are stiffened."

Ultimately, spiritual battles serve a greater purpose: they refine our faith, draw us closer to God, and allow His power to be made perfect in our weakness. Victory through Christ is not about avoiding struggles, but about standing firm in the midst of them, knowing that God is our defender. In every trial, temptation, or attack, believers can proclaim with confidence: *"The Lord will fight for you; you need only to be still."* *(Exodus 14:14, NIV)* This victory mindset transforms fear into faith, and despair into hope, offering a powerful testimony for generations to come. Through Christ, every believer has the strength to not only survive spiritual battles but to emerge victorious, shining the light of God's truth into the darkness.

THE STRUGGLE BETWEEN LIGHT AND DARKNESS

The struggle between light and darkness is not just a symbolic battle, it is a spiritual reality that has shaped human history since creation. From the moment Adam and Eve disobeyed God, sin entered the world, allowing darkness to gain a foothold in human affairs. This conflict is not limited to individual morality; it is a cosmic war between God's righteousness and the schemes of the enemy. *Ephesians 5:8 (NIV)* declares, *"For you were once darkness, but now you are light in the Lord. Live as children of light."* This verse highlights that believers are no longer slaves to sin, but they must actively walk in God's light to resist the darkness that constantly seeks to reclaim them. As John Bunyan, author of The Pilgrim's Progress, observed: "This hill, though high, I covet to ascend; the difficulty will not me offend, for I perceive the way to life lies here." This reminds us that walking in light requires intentional effort, not passive existence.

This struggle manifests in the everyday choices we make, what we think, say, and do. When faced with the temptation to lie, harbor bitterness, or compromise our faith, we are not just battling personal weakness but engaging in spiritual warfare. *Ephesians 6:12 (NIV)* confirms this: *"For our struggle is not against flesh and blood, but against the rulers, against the authorities, against the powers of this dark world and against the spiritual forces of evil in the heavenly realms."* Are these small decisions really part of a grand cosmic battle? Absolutely. Every moment we choose truth over deception, forgiveness over revenge, or purity over sin, we advance the light of God's Kingdom. Watchman Nee, The Spiritual Man famously said, "Our warfare is not conducted on the ground of hope or feeling, but on the ground of what the Lord has done." This challenges believers to recognize that every decision either strengthens their spiritual armor or leaves them vulnerable to darkness.

The consequences of losing this battle are not just personal struggles; they touch every part of life—relationships, purpose, and destiny. When people allow darkness to reign in their hearts, they drift further from

God's voice and purpose. This is evident in broken families, destructive addictions, and hopelessness that permeate society. Yet, believers are not powerless. *2 Corinthians 10:4 (NIV)* declares: *"The weapons we fight with are not the weapons of the world. On the contrary, they have divine power to demolish strongholds."* This divine power accessed through prayer, fasting, and obedience empowers Christians to break free from any bondage. Consider a man struggling with addiction who, after years of trying worldly solutions, finally surrenders his life to Christ and discovers freedom through prayer and biblical counseling; his transformation is evidence that light can shatter even the darkest chains when God's power is embraced.

It is important to understand that this battle is not reserved for moments of crisis. It is a daily, lifelong struggle that requires constant vigilance. Darkness does not wait for permission to invade; it creeps in subtly through distractions, discouragement, and spiritual laziness. This is why *1 Peter 5:8 (NIV)* warns: *"Be alert and of sober mind. Your enemy the devil prowls around like a roaring lion looking for someone to devour."* How many times have we let our guard down, assuming things are "fine," only to find ourselves trapped in fear, doubt, or compromise? As Charles Spurgeon wisely said, "The Christian life is not a playground; it is a battleground." This truth challenges both current and future generations to remain spiritually awake and armed, recognizing that complacency opens the door to the enemy's influence.

Ultimately, the struggle between light and darkness is a constant reminder that faith is not passive it is a call to action. Through Christ, victory is already secured, but believers must still fight to apply that victory in their daily lives. *John 1:5 (NIV)* offers hope: *"The light shines in the darkness, and the darkness has not overcome it."* This is both a promise and a call to courage. Future generations must learn that spiritual warfare is not a relic of the past but a present reality shaping their world. Dietrich Bonhoeffer wrote, "Discipleship is not an offer that man makes to Christ. It is Christ's call to follow, to step into the light and resist the darkness." With this understanding, believers today and tomorrow can walk boldly, not in fear of the darkness, but in confidence that God's light will always prevail.

NOTE THESE

1. Spiritual battles are real and ongoing, affecting every part of life.

2. Every choice we make either strengthens God's light in us or gives darkness a foothold.

3. Believers must remain spiritually alert and fully equipped with God's Word and prayer.

4. Victory is already secured through Christ, but we must actively walk in that victory.

5. Future generations must understand that living in God's light requires daily commitment and courage.

JESUS OUR DEFENDER IN BATTLE

Jesus is not only the Savior of our souls but also our mighty defender in the spiritual battles that rage around us. In life, we often focus on visible struggles such as financial difficulties, health crises, or relational conflicts, but Scripture reminds us that our real battle is unseen. *"For our struggle is not against flesh and blood, but against the rulers, against the authorities, against the powers of this dark world and against the spiritual forces of evil in the heavenly realms."* (Ephesians 6:12, NIV). This verse reveals that beneath the surface of our daily challenges lies a spiritual war that only Jesus, our divine defender, can help us overcome. Can human strength alone defeat an enemy we cannot see? Absolutely not. Only through the power of Jesus, who defeated sin, death, and the devil, can we find victory in these invisible battles.

Jesus' defense of His followers is rooted in His victory on the cross and His continued intercession for us today. Through His death and resurrection, Jesus disarmed every spiritual force working against believers, publicly exposing them as defeated foes. *"And having disarmed the powers and authorities, he made a public spectacle of them, triumphing over them by the cross."* (Colossians 2:15, NIV). This victory, however, is not automatic; it must be applied through faith and obedience. This truth applies not just to pastors and prophets but to every believer, from the seasoned saint to the new convert. Whether facing temptation, discouragement, or persecution, our greatest defense is the presence of Jesus, our shield and stronghold.

The divine protection of Jesus is experienced most powerfully when we actively put on the armor of God and remain under His covering. Ephesians 6:11 instructs, *"Put on the full armor of God, so that you can take your stand against the devil's schemes."* (NIV). This armor includes truth, righteousness, faith, and the Word of God tools Jesus provides to every believer. But are these spiritual weapons just religious symbols, or are they real defenses against the enemy? Consider the story of a Christian woman battling deep depression. Through prayer, Scripture meditation, and community support, she found strength and hope. Each time she declared God's truth, rejected the enemy's lies, and stood firm in faith, she experienced the defending power of Christ in action.

Furthermore, Jesus does not merely stand by and observe our battles, He actively fights for us. In John 17:15, Jesus prays for His followers, saying, *"My prayer is not that you take them out of the world but that you protect them from the evil one."* (NIV). This reveals that Jesus' defense is both spiritual and personal. He knows the unique battles each believer faces and stands as their advocate before the Father. Francis Schaeffer, The God Who Is There, wrote, "The Christian is called upon to engage in a spiritual battle, not merely to stand, but to stand against the schemes of the devil in the full armor of God." This is why the prayers of Jesus, combined with our daily surrender, are essential for overcoming the darkness we encounter in this world.

For current and future generations, the lesson is clear: spiritual battles will always exist, but victory belongs to those who trust in Jesus as their defender. In a world increasingly filled with spiritual confusion, moral compromise, and hidden attacks against faith, the need for Christ's protection is greater than ever. Just as soldiers train before war, believers must prepare daily through prayer, worship, and the Word. Whether you are a student struggling with peer pressure, a parent battling for your family's faith, or a pastor confronting opposition, remember this: *"The Lord will fight for you; you need only to be still."* (Exodus 14:14, NIV). With Jesus as our defender, no weapon formed against us will prosper, and no darkness can extinguish His light.

TRYING JESUS: THE PATH TO SPIRITUAL VICTORY

In a world filled with endless solutions and self-help strategies, trying Jesus stands out as the only path to true and lasting spiritual victory. Many individuals chase after worldly remedies, whether through wealth, fame, self-improvement books, or philosophical teachings. While these may offer temporary comfort, they cannot address the deeper spiritual void that exists in every human heart. Jesus offers something radically different not just relief from present troubles, but peace that surpasses understanding and victory that transforms the soul. *"Peace I leave with you; my peace I give you. I do not give to you as the world gives. Do not let your hearts be troubled and do not be afraid."* (John 14:27, NIV). Can any human philosophy truly offer such enduring peace? Only in Jesus do we find victory over not only external struggles but also internal battles such as fear, guilt, and hopelessness.

Trying Jesus is not a last resort but a conscious decision to surrender our lives into His capable hands. It means recognizing that human wisdom is limited, and only God's guidance can lead us to true fulfillment. Many people resist this surrender, believing they can solve their own problems, but Proverbs 3:5 reminds us to *"Trust in the Lord with all your heart and lean not on your own understanding."* (NIV). Why lean on a fragile human mind when the infinite wisdom of God is available? Renowned Christian author Jonathan Edwards, in *The Works of Jonathan Edwards*, wrote, "The enjoyment of [God] is the only happiness with which our souls can be satisfied." This treasure is available to all who are willing to try Jesus to lay down pride, confess their need for Him, and follow wherever He leads.

The decision to try Jesus leads to profound spiritual renewal and transformation. Sin creates a separation between humanity and God, leaving a void that no achievement or possession can fill. When a person places their trust in Christ, that separation is bridged, and a new identity is born. This is not merely a religious act, but a spiritual rebirth. *"Therefore, if anyone is in Christ, the new creation has come: The old has gone, the new is here!"* (2 Corinthians 5:17, NIV). Can material wealth purchase a clean conscience or eternal peace? **Can human effort erase the burden of sin? Absolutely not. Only through the blood of Jesus can a person truly experience freedom from their past and hope for their future.** This is not theoretical, countless testimonies from former addicts, criminals, and broken souls testify to the renewing power of trying Jesus.

Trying Jesus also prepares believers to face life's inevitable challenges with courage and hope. Following Christ does not exempt one from trials, but it provides the strength and perspective to endure them. Jesus Himself said, *"In this world you will have trouble. But take heart! I have overcome the world."* (John 16:33, NIV). This is a critical truth for both current and future generations. Many today seek quick fixes and instant gratification, but spiritual victory is forged through endurance, prayer, and unwavering faith in Christ. As J.I. Packer once wrote, "If you want to judge how well a person understands Christianity, find out how much he makes of the thought of being God's child, and having God as his Father." Packer reminds us that the foundation of Christian faith is the intimate trust we have in God as our Father, which provides unwavering assurance through every storm and uncertainty we face in life. For both current and future generations, the lesson is clear: there is no better time to try Jesus than now. Procrastination is one of the enemy's most effective weapons, convincing people they have plenty of time to turn to God. But why delay when Jesus stands ready to receive anyone who comes to Him? *"Here I am! I stand at the door and knock. If anyone hears my voice and opens the door, I will come in and eat with that person, and they with me."* (Revelation 3:20, NIV). This invitation is open to all young and old, rich and poor, educated and uneducated. Whether you are a struggling student, a broken parent, or a successful professional seeking deeper meaning, the path to spiritual victory begins with trying Jesus. And once you do, you will discover a love and peace that the world can never give, and that no circumstance can take away.

NOTE THESE

1. True and lasting victory in life comes only through trusting Jesus, not through human wisdom or worldly solutions.

2. Surrendering to Jesus leads to spiritual transformation, offering freedom from sin and a new identity in Christ.

3. Following Jesus prepares believers to endure life's challenges with courage, peace, and unwavering hope.

4. Delaying to try Jesus is dangerous because the opportunity to receive His salvation and guidance should never be postponed.

5. Jesus' invitation is open to all people, regardless of their background, making Him the ultimate source of spiritual victory for every generation.

CHAPTER FIVE

JESUS, THE ANSWER TO LIFE'S BURDENS

Life presents burdens that touch everyone, regardless of status, wealth, or background. Stress, pain, uncertainty, and brokenness are universal human experiences, yet many people seek relief in temporary solutions such as wealth, relationships, or distractions like entertainment. However, these comforts quickly fade, leaving the soul even emptier than before. Is there a lasting solution to these burdens? *Jesus offers the only answer that brings true peace and rest.* As He invites in *Matthew 11:28-30 (NIV): "Come to me, all you who are weary and burdened, and I will give you rest…For my yoke is easy and my burden is light."* **Unlike worldly remedies that require self-sufficiency, Jesus asks only for our willingness to come, no qualifications needed.**

The burdens of life come in many forms, such as emotional wounds, financial stress, physical sickness, and spiritual emptiness. Some burdens stem from past mistakes, while others arise from circumstances beyond our control. Society often teaches self-reliance: "work harder," "think positively," or "fix it yourself." But what happens when strength fails, and positivity runs out? King David, who faced heavy burdens himself, pointed to a better way in *Psalm 55:22 (NIV): "Cast your cares on the Lord and he will sustain you; he will never let the righteous be shaken."* This profound truth shifts the focus from self to surrender offering our burdens to God instead of trying to carry them alone. After all, if the Creator of the universe offers to help, why would anyone refuse?

Unlike temporary relief, Jesus offers rest that reaches the soul. His rest is not just the absence of problems but the presence of peace in the midst of them. Surrendering to Jesus does not mean life becomes perfect, but it means the burdens we carry are now shared with Him. *Isaiah 41:10 (NIV) reassures us: "So do not fear, for I am with you; do not be dismayed, for I am your God. I will strengthen you and help you; I will uphold you with my righteous right hand."* This promise is not for the strong or the deserving, but for anyone humble enough to admit their need. C.S. Lewis wrote, "Relying on God has to begin all over again every day as if nothing had yet been done." This daily reliance is how true rest is experienced.

Some may wonder, "Is it really that simple just come to Jesus?" The world complicates the process, offering countless alternatives, but Jesus keeps it clear: *"Come."* Even today, many testimonies exist of people who tried everything else and found their only lasting peace in Christ. Consider a man overwhelmed by financial ruin who turned to alcohol for escape, only to find himself deeper in despair. Yet, after surrendering his life to Christ, he discovered a peace that remained even while his finances slowly recovered. Jesus did not magically erase his debts, but He lifted the greater burden, the weight of hopelessness.

For both current and future generations, the lesson is clear: burdens are inevitable but carrying them alone is optional. Jesus offers to walk alongside every person willing to trust Him. The next generation, faced with new pressures and uncertainties, must remember this timeless truth: self-reliance only goes so far, but Christ-reliance leads to rest for the soul. *John 14:27 (NIV) declares: "Peace I leave with you; my peace I give you. I do not give to you as the world gives. Do not let your hearts be troubled and do not be afraid."* This divine peace is not the absence of storms but the calm assurance that Jesus holds the storm in His hands. The greatest gift any generation can leave for the next is the example of fully trusting Jesus, the true answer to life's burdens.

JESUS, THE ONLY SURE FOUNDATION

Life's storms come in manifest in various ways: wars, economic crises, sickness, heartbreak, and emotional distress. In the face of such trials, people naturally search for stability and peace. Some look to wealth, believing money will protect them. Others turn to relationships, hoping companionship will fill the void. **Still, others pursue fame and success, thinking achievements will secure their legacy. But do these things truly satisfy?** Time and time again, they fail to bring lasting peace. *Jesus alone offers a foundation that cannot be shaken.* As He assures in *John 14:27 (NIV), "Peace I leave with you; my peace I give you. I do not give to you as the world gives. Do not let your hearts be troubled and do not be afraid."* This peace is not circumstantial; it flows directly from God's unchanging nature, providing strength in the middle of chaos.

Beyond offering peace, Jesus brings enduring hope. In a world where the future is uncertain and fear grips many hearts, Christ stands as a beacon of purpose and promise. *Jeremiah 29:11 (NIV) declares, "For I know the plans I have for you," declares the Lord, "plans to prosper you and not to harm you, plans to give you hope and a future."* Can any human plan offer such assurance? The world's promises often collapse under pressure, but God's promises stand eternal. Charles Spurgeon said, "To trust God in the light is nothing, but trust Him in the dark, that is faith." This hope sustains both individuals and entire generations, giving meaning even to suffering because every moment is part of God's redemptive plan.

In times of conflict and struggle, Jesus also acts as our defender. Many believe they must fight every battle alone, using their own wisdom and strength. Yet Scripture teaches otherwise. *Exodus 14:14 (NIV) proclaims, "The Lord will fight for you; you need only to be still."* What a profound truth, victory does not depend on our strength but on our surrender to God's power. Consider a person unjustly accused at work, tempted to retaliate. When they choose instead to trust God and respond with integrity, they often witness divine intervention, proving that God indeed fights for His own.

When burdens grow too heavy to bear, Jesus invites us to lay them down at His feet. The world teaches self-reliance: "Be strong," "Keep pushing," "You've got this." But what if strength runs out? *Psalm 55:22 (NIV) urges, "Cast your cares on the Lord and he will sustain you; he will never let the righteous be shaken."* True strength comes not from within but from the One who holds all things together. Imagine a single mother drowning in financial and emotional stress. As she kneels in prayer, surrendering her fears to Jesus, peace fills her heart despite no immediate change in circumstances. This is the mystery of divine rest, burdens lifted not by removal but by the comforting presence of Christ.

Perhaps the greatest reason Jesus is the only sure foundation is His unchanging nature. In a world where values, governments, and even relationships shift constantly, Jesus remains eternally reliable. *Hebrews 13:8 (NIV) boldly declares, "Jesus Christ is the same yesterday and today and forever."* This truth is an anchor for all generations. Today's youth may face technological advancements and cultural pressures, but they need the same unshakable foundation that sustained their ancestors. For future generations, the lesson is clear: Build your life on Christ, and no storm will destroy you. As the hymn writer Edward Mote penned, "On Christ the solid rock I stand, all other ground is sinking sand." Whether in times of peace or peril, Jesus remains the only foundation that will never fail.

NOTE THESE

1. Build your life on Jesus, not on wealth, success, or relationships.

2. Trust God's plans, even when the future seems uncertain.

3. Allow God to fight your battles instead of seeking revenge.

4. Surrender your burdens to Jesus instead of carrying them alone.

5. Remember, Jesus is the only foundation that never changes.

A MIGHTY MAN IN NEED OF JESUS

Naaman's story is a powerful reminder that no amount of human greatness can shield us from life's deepest struggles. Despite his military success, wealth, and influence, Naaman could not conquer the disease of leprosy on his own. His armor hid the physical shame, but nothing could remove the internal burden he carried. *2 Kings 5:1 (NIV)* states, *"Now Naaman was commander of the army of the king of Aram. He was a great man in the sight of his master and highly regarded, because through him the Lord had given victory to Aram. He was a valiant soldier, but he had leprosy."* Isn't this a reflection of many lives today, people who appear strong, successful, and celebrated in public but privately battle sickness, addiction, loneliness, or guilt? This teaches that external success does not exempt anyone from the need for divine help.

One striking truth from Naaman's story is that human pride often stands in the way of divine solutions. When the prophet Elisha instructed Naaman to wash in the humble Jordan River, Naaman was insulted. He expected a dramatic display fitting his high status. *2 Kings 5:11-12 (NIV)* says, *"But Naaman went away angry and said, 'I thought that he would surely come out to me and stand and call on the name of the Lord his God, wave his hand over the spot and cure me of my leprosy. Are not Abana and Pharpar, the rivers of Damascus, better than all the waters of Israel?'"* How often do we miss God's blessings because they come in ways we do not expect? Andrew Murray wisely affirmed, "Humility is nothing but the disappearance of self in the vision that God is all." Only after Naaman humbled himself did healing flow, showing that God's power often requires our surrender.

Naaman's healing also highlights the importance of obedience, even when God's instructions seem too simple or ordinary. The prophet's command to wash in the Jordan River seven times seemed beneath the dignity of a mighty commander. Yet, God's power works through faith and obedience, not through human logic. *2 Kings 5:14 (NIV)* records, *"So he went down and dipped himself in the Jordan seven times, as the man of God had told him, and his flesh was restored and became clean like that of a young boy."* Isn't this a reminder that God's miracles often begin with simple acts of faith? In the words of Oswald Chambers, "Faith never knows where it is being led, but it loves and knows the One who is leading."

Naaman's transformation is also spiritual, not just physical. His healing led him to acknowledge the God of Israel as the one true God. Before his encounter with Elisha, Naaman relied on his power and position. After his healing, he declared faith in God. *2 Kings 5:15 (NIV)* says, *"Now I know that there is no God in all the world except in Israel."* This is the ultimate healing recognizing that life's purpose is not in earthly success but in knowing and serving the living God. Practical examples of this truth are everywhere. Think of a wealthy businessman who has everything money can buy but feels empty until he encounters Jesus at a prayer meeting. His financial success fades in importance compared to the peace and purpose found in Christ.

NOTE THESE

1. True success includes knowing Jesus, not just achieving wealth or fame.

2. Pride can block divine blessings; humility opens the door to miracles.

3. Obedience, even in small matters, invites God's power into our lives.

4. Physical healing is temporary, but the spiritual transformation is eternal.

5. Never judge anyone by their outward success; everyone needs Jesus.

THE POWER OF HUMILITY IN RECEIVING GOD'S BLESSINGS

Humility is a key that unlocks the door to divine blessings, yet it is often overlooked in a world that celebrates power, achievement, and self-sufficiency. Many people believe that blessings are earned through hard work, intelligence, or influence. However, Scripture teaches that God's favor often flows to those who humbly recognize their need for Him. *"Humble yourselves before the Lord, and he will lift you up"* (James

4:10, NIV). This means that human strength alone cannot secure the blessings that come from above; only a heart that bows in surrender before God is truly positioned to receive His grace and favor.

From a different perspective, some argue that self-confidence and personal ambition are the pathways to success. Society promotes the idea that people must fight for their blessings and rely on their own wisdom to succeed. Yet, the Bible presents a contrasting view. God resists the proud but gives grace to the humble. *"God opposes the proud but shows favor to the humble"* (1 Peter 5:5, NIV). When people rely solely on their own abilities, they risk closing their hearts to the miraculous interventions that come only through God's hand. Rick Warren, in Mere Christianity, wrote, "True humility is not thinking less of yourself; it is thinking of yourself less and thinking of others more." True humility does not mean denying personal abilities, but rather acknowledging that every gift, every opportunity, and every blessing ultimately comes from God.

The story of Naaman, a mighty commander afflicted with leprosy, illustrates this truth in a profound way. Despite his power, wealth, and influence, his healing only came when he humbled himself and obeyed the prophet Elisha's simple instruction to wash in the Jordan River. Initially, Naaman's pride almost robbed him of his miracle. He expected a dramatic, honor-worthy cure that matched his status. However, his breakthrough came only after he laid down his pride and chose humble obedience. *"So, he went down and dipped himself in the Jordan seven times... and his flesh was restored and became clean like that of a young boy"* (2 Kings 5:14, NIV). Naaman's story teaches that pride blocks blessings, but humility opens the floodgates of God's healing and restoration.

What about today? Many people, especially those in high positions of authority, struggle to acknowledge their dependence on God. A successful business leader may believe their wealth came entirely from their intelligence and effort. However, when sudden illness strikes or unforeseen challenges arise, they are reminded of their human frailty. Consider a wealthy entrepreneur diagnosed with a terminal disease. No amount of money or influence can purchase healing. In desperation, the entrepreneur turns to Christ, prays humbly, and experiences both physical and spiritual restoration. This modern example mirrors Naaman's story, showing that divine blessings often follow genuine humility. *"Blessed are the poor in spirit, for theirs is the kingdom of heaven"* (Matthew 5:3, NIV).

For future generations, the lesson is clear: humility positions us to receive from God in ways pride never can. In a culture obsessed with self-promotion and personal glory, the Bible calls us to a different path, the path of surrender, dependence, and humble obedience. Andrew Murray wrote, "Pride must die in you, or nothing of heaven can live in you." As young people pursue careers, relationships, and personal dreams, they must remember that lasting success and true blessings come not from human striving but from humble submission to God's will. Humility is not weakness; it is the posture that attracts divine strength, wisdom, and favor.

NOTE THESE

1. True blessings from God flow to those who approach Him with humility, not pride.

2. Human strength, wealth, or status cannot replace the need for divine help and guidance.

3. Pride blocks the flow of God's blessings, while humble obedience opens the door to miracles.

4. Humility teaches us to recognize that every success is a gift from God, not a product of personal effort alone.

5. Future generations must learn that true greatness comes from surrendering to God, not from self-promotion.

6

CHAPTER SIX

WEALTH AND POWER COULD NOT BRING TRUE HEALING

Wealth and power refer to the possession of material riches, financial resources, and the ability to influence others or control situations. Wealth allows individuals to access luxury, comfort, and opportunities, while power gives them authority and control over decisions and people. Together, wealth and power often create a sense of security and importance. However, history and human experience show that wealth and power alone cannot guarantee true happiness, peace, or inner fulfillment. While they may solve external problems, they are powerless in addressing deeper spiritual and emotional needs.

Naaman's story presents a deep reality that remains relevant today, wealth and power cannot purchase true healing or inner peace. As commander of the Syrian army, Naaman stood at the pinnacle of success, commanding respect, wealth, and influence. **Yet beneath the armor of his accomplishments lay an incurable disease, leprosy, which no human effort could cure.** This reflects the reality that, no matter how much wealth or fame a person acquires, certain struggles, spiritual emptiness, emotional pain, or physical ailments lie beyond the reach of human solutions. *Proverbs 11:4 (NIV) reminds us: "Wealth is worthless in the day of wrath, but righteousness delivers from death."* Earthly riches can only address temporary needs, but true healing flows from God alone.

From a modern perspective, many people walk in Naaman's shoes. They excel in business, politics, or entertainment yet suffer silently behind closed doors. Celebrities check into rehab despite having fortune and fame; successful entrepreneurs battle loneliness and depression despite their achievements. This raises a critical question: *If wealth and power bring happiness, why do so many wealthy individuals suffer quietly?* As John Piper famously wrote, **"God is most glorified in us when we are most satisfied in Him."** Piper's words echo the truth that deep and lasting satisfaction, true healing of the soul, can only be found in God, not in worldly pursuits or temporary comforts.

Naaman's healing journey also highlights the importance of humility and obedience. When the prophet Elisha instructed him to wash seven times in the Jordan River, Naaman was offended. He expected a grand ceremony, perhaps something fitting for his rank. Yet, God's way is often simple but requires faith and surrender. *2 Kings 5:13 (NIV) records his servant's wise advice: "My father, if the prophet had told you to do some great thing, would you not have done it? How much more then, when he tells you, 'Wash and be cleansed'!"* This teaches a powerful lesson, God's solutions are often unexpected, but they lead to lasting transformation when followed with faith.

This principle is still true today. People chase after elaborate solutions, expensive therapies, luxurious retreats, or self-help programs, all in search of inner peace and healing. But like Naaman, true healing is found in simple, sincere faith in God. *Psalm 147:3 (NIV) declares: "He heals the brokenhearted and binds up their wounds."* Whether it is a broken heart, a tormented mind, or an incurable disease, true healing comes when we humble ourselves before God and trust His process, even if it seems too simple or unconventional by worldly standards.

For future generations, the story of Naaman serves as both a warning and an invitation. The warning is clear, trusting in wealth, status, or human solutions alone will always fall short. The invitation is even clearer, God offers healing, peace, and purpose to anyone willing to surrender to Him. A practical example can be seen in the life of John Newton, who, after encountering Christ, found both forgiveness and purpose, penned the famous hymn "Amazing Grace," testifying that true healing and freedom come not from human success, but from God's grace. Future generations must learn that real wealth lies not in material possessions but in a life surrendered to Christ, the true source of healing and peace.

HUMILITY AND OBEDIENCE LEAD TO GOD'S BLESSINGS

Naaman's story teaches a timeless truth: God often works through simple acts of humility and obedience rather than grand displays of power. Naaman, a highly respected military commander, was used to commands and strategies fitting his status. But when Elisha told him to wash in the humble waters of the Jordan River, Naaman was offended. He expected something more dramatic, something that matched his position. This reaction reflects how human pride can block divine blessings. *"God opposes the proud but shows favor to the humble"* (James 4:6, NIV). Only after Naaman humbled himself and obeyed was his healing released. This shows that God's blessings flow not through pride but through surrender.

This principle is not unique to Naaman; it runs through the Bible. Consider Joshua and the Israelites at Jericho. They did not conquer the city through military power but through obedience to God's unusual instruction to march around the walls (Joshua 6). Similarly, Peter, a professional fisherman, only caught an abundance of fish after obeying Jesus' command to cast his net again, despite his initial doubts (Luke 5:5-6). These examples show that God's blessings often come through obedience that defies human logic. As *Isaiah 55:8-9 (NIV)* reminds us:

"For my thoughts are not your thoughts, neither are your ways my ways." God's ways are higher than ours, and blessings often lie beyond our understanding.

Yet many today struggle with the simplicity of God's instructions. Some believe that salvation must be earned through good works or religious rituals, rather than accepting the simple truth that faith in Jesus brings salvation. *"If you declare with your mouth, 'Jesus is Lord,' and believe in your heart that God raised him from the dead, you will be saved"* (Romans 10:9, NIV). Others hesitate to obey God's call to forgive, to give generously, or to serve humbly, thinking it makes them vulnerable. However, obedience always positions us for God's provision and protection. *"Blessed are all who fear the Lord, who walk in obedience to him"* (Psalm 128:1, NIV).

Christian literature also echoes this truth. Andrew Murray wrote, "Humility is the path to the deeper life with God. It is the place of entire dependence on Him." Obedience without humility becomes legalism, but humility without obedience is incomplete surrender. True faith blends both humbly accepting God's will and acting upon it. This applies to every generation, teaching that human logic, pride, and personal achievements can never replace simple trust in God's wisdom. Today's success-driven culture often overlooks this, but those who learn to listen and obey God's voice will always experience His blessings.

A practical example is seen in business leaders who submit their work to God, asking for His guidance instead of relying solely on market trends. One entrepreneur, after years of chasing profits, finally prayed for direction and felt led to close on Sundays to honor God. Despite fears of financial loss, the business flourished beyond expectations. Like Naaman, this person's blessing came through humility and obedience. This lesson stands for current and future generations: God's blessings are not reserved for the powerful or the wealthy but are given to those willing to trust and obey His word. As Naaman's story reveals, sometimes the simplest steps of faith unlock the greatest miracles.

NOTE THESE

1. True blessings from God come through humility and obedience, not through wealth, power, or personal achievements.

2. God's instructions may seem simple or unusual, but they always lead to the best outcomes when followed in faith.

3. Pride can block God's blessings, but humility opens the door to divine healing and restoration.

4. Obedience to God's word often requires trusting Him even when His ways do not make logical sense.

5. Every generation must learn that God's blessings are not earned through human effort, but received through humble surrender and faithful obedience.

NO ONE IS SAFE WITHOUT JESUS

In a world filled with uncertainty, wars, financial instability, and personal struggles, people often seek safety and security in the wrong places. Many trust in governments, wealth, or influential connections, believing these will shield them from life's troubles. However, history proves that even the mightiest empires crumble and the richest people face crises that money cannot solve. The Bible makes this truth clear in *Psalm 20:7 (NIV): "Some trust in chariots and some in horses, but we trust in the name of the Lord our God."* True safety cannot be built on human systems, because they are fragile and temporary. Jesus alone offers lasting security that transcends human understanding.

Without Jesus, people are not only physically vulnerable but also spiritually exposed. They may appear successful in the eyes of the world, yet deep within, they battle fear, anxiety, and emptiness. What good is wealth when it cannot buy peace? What use is power when it cannot silence the storms of the soul? *John 14:6 (NIV) reminds us of Jesus' words: "I am the way and the truth and the life. No one comes to the Father except through me."* True safety is not just about surviving today but securing eternity. Without Jesus, no one can stand firm when life's ultimate tests come.

Some might argue that hard work, education, and careful planning offer sufficient security. While these things are valuable, they cannot shield anyone from unexpected illness, personal loss, or death itself. *Matthew 6:34 (NIV) teaches: "Therefore do not worry about tomorrow, for tomorrow will worry about itself. Each day has enough trouble of its own."* This is not a call to laziness but a reminder that no amount of human effort can guarantee absolute safety. Trusting Jesus does not remove life's difficulties, but it ensures that we never face them alone.

Even for believers, life brings storms, but they face those storms with divine strength. Their foundation is built not on wealth or influence but on Christ, the Rock. *Psalm 91:2 (NIV) boldly declares: "I will say of the Lord, 'He is my refuge and my fortress, my God, in whom I trust.'"* This confidence comes not from a trouble-free life but from knowing that Jesus is always present, offering peace that passes understanding. Imagine two people caught in the same storm, one stands on shifting sand, and the other stands on solid rock. The one on the rock may still feel the wind, but they will not fall.

For current and future generations, this is a critical lesson: the world will always be unstable, but Jesus is forever faithful. Technology will advance, economies will rise and fall, and global crises will come and go. However, Jesus remains the same yesterday, today, and forever (Hebrews 13:8). True safety is not about avoiding danger but knowing who holds you in His hands. Those who choose to build their lives on Jesus, the unshakable foundation, will discover that in Him alone, they are truly safe.

HEALING FROM THE LEPROSY OF LIFE

In today's world, many people seem to have it all wealth, power, influence, and admiration. Yet beneath the surface, they silently battle with internal struggles that no amount of success can erase. This is the modern equivalent of Naaman's condition. *2 Kings 5:1 (NIV) states: "Now Naaman was commander of the army of the king of Aram. He was a great man in the sight of his master and highly regarded, because through him the Lord had given victory to Aram. He was a valiant soldier, but he had leprosy."* Just like Naaman's visible success could not hide his hidden suffering, many today wear smiles in public but cry in private. What good is external success when the soul is plagued with guilt, fear, addiction, or emptiness? John Bunyan wrote, "What God says is best, is best, though all the men in the world are against it."

Naaman's leprosy is a picture of sin, the greatest spiritual disease humanity faces. Sin separates us from God, leaving us spiritually disfigured, no matter how polished we appear on the outside. *Romans 3:23 (NIV) confirms this truth: "For all have sinned and fall short of the glory of God."* Wealth cannot purchase forgiveness, and power cannot demand it. What human invention can wash away guilt? What earthly authority can guarantee eternal peace? Just as Naaman could not heal himself, no human being can cleanse their own heart from sin. This challenges the common belief that good deeds, religious observance, or personal achievement can make someone right with God. True healing comes only from divine grace.

Naaman's healing came not through wealth or royal favor but through humility and obedience to God's word. The prophet Elisha gave a simple instruction: wash seven times in the Jordan River. Naaman almost refused because the solution seemed too ordinary. He expected a grand ceremony fitting for his status. *2 Kings 5:13-14 (NIV) records his servants' wise counsel: "My father, if the prophet had told you to do some great thing, would you not have done it? How much more then, when he tells you, 'Wash and be cleansed'!"* This reveals a powerful truth: God's solutions often require simple faith, not complex rituals. Many today miss out on spiritual healing because they seek dramatic experiences or believe salvation must be earned through effort.

The lessons from Naaman's story still speak to our generation and those to come. First, outward success does not mean inward peace. Second, true healing comes only through humble obedience to God's word. Third, God's way of salvation through faith in Jesus Christ may seem simple, but it is the only way. *John 14:6 (NIV) reminds us: "I am the way and the truth and the life. No one comes to the Father except through me."* Future generations must learn that no career achievement, social status, or personal wealth can replace a healed and forgiven heart. Just as Naaman found his cure in God's power, so every person must come humbly to Jesus, the only true source of healing for the "leprosy" of sin.

JESUS CLEANSES THE "LEPROSY" OF SIN

Sin, much like a disease, corrupts every area of life spiritually, emotionally, and even physically. It builds an invisible wall between humanity and God, leaving people burdened with guilt and shame. Some may try to cover up their inner brokenness through wealth, fame, or acts of charity, but none of these can cleanse the soul. *1 John 1:9 (NIV) assures us: "If we confess our sins, he is faithful and just and will forgive us our sins and purify us from all unrighteousness."* Just as a person like Naaman needed divine healing, every sinner needed divine cleansing. Why do so many resist this simple truth? Is it pride, fear, or believing that their sins are too great for forgiveness? Yet, time and again, Scripture proves that no sin is beyond the reach of God's mercy.

Throughout history, humanity has clung to the idea that salvation can be earned through good deeds. People believe that generous donations, moral living, or religious rituals can wash away sin. However, the Bible teaches otherwise. *Ephesians 2:8-9 (NIV) clearly states: "For it is by grace you have been saved, through faith, and this is not from yourselves, it is the gift of God, not by works, so that no one can boast."* This truth humbles even the most religious among us. As Martin Luther wrote, "The law discovers the disease. The gospel gives the remedy." Luther powerfully reminds us that **human effort, through law-keeping or moral striving, only reveals our brokenness**, but grace through Jesus is the only cure.

The world constantly offers substitutes for true peace, money, power, entertainment, even relationships, but none of these can heal the disease of sin. *Mark 8:36 (NIV) asks: "What good is it for someone to gain the whole world, yet forfeit their soul?"* **What is the price of a soul? King Solomon, who possessed unmatched wealth and wisdom, eventually confessed the emptiness of life apart from God (Ecclesiastes 1:2).** True peace only comes when we humble ourselves and admit our need for Jesus. *Proverbs 3:5-6 (NIV) advises: "Trust in the Lord with all your heart and lean not on your own understanding; in all your ways submit to him, and he will make your paths straight."* What holds people back from trusting Jesus fully? Often, it is pride the same pride that kept Naaman from initially obeying Elisha's simple command to wash in the Jordan.

For anyone burdened with guilt, pain, or regret, Jesus stands ready to cleanse and restore. *Isaiah 1:18 (NIV) declares: "Come now, let us settle the matter," says the Lord. "Though your sins are like scarlet, they shall be as white as snow."* This is not just a poetic promise; it is the heart of the gospel. No sin is too dark, no past too broken, for the cleansing blood of Jesus. This divine exchange is the very essence of grace He takes our sin, and we receive His righteousness.

This truth carries vital lessons for both this generation and those yet to come. First, outward success can never cleanse inward sin. Second, salvation cannot be earned but must be humbly received. Third, substitutes like wealth, fame, or distraction only delay the inevitable confrontation with the emptiness of sin. Finally, true peace comes only through the cleansing power of Jesus Christ. Future generations must learn that the pursuit of worldly success without spiritual cleansing is like dressing a leper in fine clothes, it may hide the symptoms for a time, but only Jesus can heal the disease. As you reflect on these truths, ask yourself: Have I allowed Jesus to cleanse my heart, or am I still trying to cover my wounds with temporary solutions? The choice is yours, but the invitation stands, let Jesus cleanse you today.

THE HIDDEN LEPROSY IN OUR LIVES

In biblical times, leprosy was not just a disease that affected the skin; it was a mark of separation, shame, and hopelessness. Those diagnosed with it were cast out of society, forced to live isolated and unclean. However, the deeper message of leprosy extends beyond the physical, it reflects the condition of the human heart weighed down by sin, guilt, and brokenness. Today, while physical leprosy is rare, **there is a hidden leprosy that affects countless lives a spiritual and emotional leprosy hidden beneath polished appearances and forced smiles.** *Isaiah 59:2 (NIV) declares: "But your iniquities have separated you from your God; your sins have hidden his face from you, so that he will not hear."* Just like ancient lepers were cut off from society, sin cuts humanity off from God, leaving a void that no earthly solution can fill.

This hidden leprosy manifests in many forms: secret addictions, unresolved trauma, deep-seated bitterness, and the crushing weight of unforgiveness. Outwardly, many appear successful, smiling in public while silently battling private pain. Some seek relief through alcohol, drugs, pornography, or gambling. Others achieve wealth, power, or fame, yet remain restless inside. Can outward success truly mask internal brokenness? **Why do so many people who seem to "have it all" still battle emptiness, anxiety, and despair?** *Psalm 34:18 (NIV) offers comfort: "The Lord is close to the brokenhearted and saves those who are crushed in spirit."* This verse reminds us that God sees beyond appearances He reaches into the hidden places where human suffering resides.

The world teaches that money, fame, and achievements bring happiness, yet reality paints a different picture. **We see wealthy celebrities battling depression, famous influencers confessing to inner emptiness, and powerful leaders consumed by anxiety.** *Mark 8:36 (NIV) asks: "What good is it for someone to gain the whole world, yet forfeit their soul?"* This rhetorical question strikes at the heart of modern society's misplaced priorities. Christian author A.W. Tozer once said, *"The will of God is not something you add to your life. It's a course you choose. You either line* *yourself up with the Word of God or you capitulate to the principle which governs the rest of the world."* This quote reminds us that **God's will is not a side option but the true direction for a healed purposeful life.** Outside of it, no treasure can satisfy.

Naaman's story provides a profound lesson. Though he was a respected military commander, his leprosy humbled him. No amount of wealth, influence, or military victories could cure him. His healing came only when he obeyed the prophet Elisha's instruction to wash in the Jordan River a seemingly simple act that required great humility. *2 Kings 5:14 (NIV) records: "So he went down and dipped himself in the Jordan seven times, as the man of God had told him, and his flesh was restored and became clean like that of a young boy."* How often do we, like Naaman, resist God's way because it seems too simple or because it challenges our pride? **True healing begins when pride ends, and surrender starts.** Oswald Chambers wrote, "We have to pray with our eyes on God, not on the difficulties."

For today's and future generations; First, outward success can never heal inward brokenness. Second, **God's healing often requires humility, obedience, and surrender.** Third, pursuing worldly solutions for spiritual problems will always leave people empty. Fourth, **Jesus offers complete healing to all who come to Him, no matter how deep the wound.** *Matthew 11:28 (NIV) invites: "Come to me, all you who are weary and burdened, and I will give you rest."* Finally, the greatest danger is ignoring the hidden leprosy of sin and pretending everything is fine. **Future generations must understand that ignoring inner wounds does not heal them only Jesus, the Great Physician, can cleanse, restore, and make whole.** Will you surrender your hidden leprosy to Him today?

ONLY JESUS CAN HEAL THE HIDDEN LEPROSY

The world offers countless remedies for inner pain therapy, self-help books, wealth, relationships, and achievements but none of these can fully heal the wounds hidden deep within the human heart. **Only Jesus,**

the Great Physician, can cleanse the soul of its hidden leprosy the spiritual sickness caused by sin, guilt, fear, and shame. Like Naaman, who suffered from physical leprosy despite his wealth and military success, many today live with hidden struggles that no amount of money, fame, or human wisdom can cure. *John 14:6 (NIV) reminds us of the only true solution: "I am the way and the truth and the life. No one comes to the Father except through me."* This verse highlights that healing, reconciliation, and ultimate peace can only come through Christ.

Naaman's story reflects a truth that transcends time: pride often blocks the path to healing. When Elisha told Naaman to wash seven times in the Jordan River, Naaman was offended. He expected a dramatic miracle, perhaps involving rituals or powerful displays of divine power. **How often do people today expect God to work according to their terms, only to reject the simple act of surrendering to His will?** *2 Kings 5:14 (NIV) records: "So he went down and dipped himself in the Jordan seven times, as the man of God had told him, and his flesh was restored and became clean like that of a young boy."* His healing came not from wealth or position, but from obedience and humility.

Many people today pursue wealth, relationships, career success, and even religious rituals hoping these will heal their inner emptiness. But these external efforts, while sometimes helpful, cannot cure the disease of the soul. **Only Jesus, through His grace and forgiveness, can cleanse the heart and restore true peace.** *Isaiah 1:18 (NIV) offers hope: "Come now, let us settle the matter, says the Lord. Though your sins are like scarlet, they shall be as white as snow."* This divine invitation reminds us that no one is too broken or sinful to be restored by the mercy of God. No matter how far someone has fallen, Jesus stands ready to cleanse and restore.

The burdens of life, past mistakes, secret sins, and unresolved pain can weigh heavily on the human heart, like an invisible leprosy eating away at joy and hope. Yet Jesus invites all who are weary to come to Him for rest. *Matthew 11:28 (NIV) says: "Come to me, all you who are weary and burdened, and I will give you rest."* This rest is more than temporary comfort it is the deep healing that only God's forgiveness, love, and presence can provide. **When we stop hiding our wounds and surrender them to Jesus, we find freedom that no earthly solution can offer.**

For current and future generations, the lesson is clear: **Do not seek healing in places that can only offer temporary relief; turn to the One who can heal the soul.** True healing comes not through prideful self-sufficiency, but through humble surrender to Jesus Christ. His love reaches every wound, His grace covers every sin, and His power restores what sin and life have broken. **The hidden leprosy of the heart can only be cleansed by the blood of Jesus.** Will this generation and those to come continue to chase worldly cures, or will they turn to the eternal healer who offers life, hope, and restoration? The choice remains ours, but the invitation stands open.

NOTE THESE

1. True healing comes only from Jesus, not from wealth, success, or human effort.

2. Pride can block us from receiving God's healing, but humility and obedience open the door to restoration.

3. No sin is too great for God's mercy, and no wound is too deep for His healing.

4. Jesus invites all who are weary and broken to come to Him for rest and peace.

5. Future generations must learn to seek God first, trusting His way rather than relying on temporary worldly solutions.

7

CHAPTER SEVEN

THE ILLUSION OF SUCCESS WITHOUT JESUS

The story of King Solomon provides a deep reflection on the illusion of success without God. Solomon was the wealthiest and wisest king of his time, known for his grandeur, riches, and vast achievements. Yet despite all this, Solomon himself admitted that life without God is meaningless. In Ecclesiastes 1:2 (NIV), Solomon declares: *"Meaningless! Meaningless! says the Teacher. Utterly meaningless! Everything is meaningless."* This confession reveals that wealth, wisdom, and power could not satisfy the deep longing of his soul. **This same truth applies today no matter how successful a person appears, without Jesus, their heart remains restless and their soul remains unclean.**

When we look at today's world, the same story plays out in countless lives. Many celebrities, wealthy business moguls, and influential leaders appear to have it all. Yet behind the fame and fortune, many struggle with depression, broken relationships, and spiritual emptiness. Why? Because success built on worldly achievements alone is a fragile illusion. As Jesus asked in Mark 8:36 (NIV), *"What good is it for someone to gain the whole world, yet forfeit their soul?"* This rhetorical question challenges us to reflect what is the true value of success if it leaves our spirit sick and distant from God. St. Augustine rightly said, "You have made us for yourself, O Lord, and our hearts are restless until they rest in you."

Solomon, despite all his wealth and wisdom, fell into this trap when he allowed his heart to drift from God. He pursued countless pleasures, accumulated treasures, and built magnificent palaces, yet none of these things could satisfy the emptiness inside. This teaches us that **true fulfillment is not found in material possessions or earthly achievements but in walking closely with God.** In Proverbs 3:5-6 (NIV), Solomon himself gave this advice: *"Trust in the Lord with all your heart and lean not on your own understanding; in all your ways submit to him, and he will make your paths straight."* His life serves as both a testimony and a warning: chasing success without God leads to spiritual ruin.

Even today, many people believe that working harder, earning more, and achieving fame will bring lasting happiness. But every story of a fallen celebrity, every testimony of a wealthy person who feels empty, proves otherwise. The world offers temporary satisfaction, but only Jesus offers lasting peace. Jesus invites all who are weary and burdened to come to Him, saying in Matthew 11:28 (NIV), *"Come to me, all you who are weary and burdened, and I will give you rest."* True success is not measured by earthly standards but by the peace and purpose found in Christ.

For future generations, the lesson is clear: do not be deceived by the illusion of worldly success. Learn from Solomon's journey that apart from God, even the highest achievements are hollow. True success is not in what we own but in who we belong to. A.W. Tozer wrote, *"The man who has God for his treasure has all things in One."* This is the truth that must guide not only this generation but every generation to come.

OBEY HIS WORD

Obedience to God's Word is a central theme throughout the Bible, yet many people still struggle to follow it. Why do so many resist the very instructions designed to bring them peace and restoration? In today's world, human reasoning, personal ambition, and worldly philosophies often overshadow the clear teachings of Scripture. People seek answers in self-help books, social media advice, and personal experiences, forgetting that **true wisdom comes from obeying the One who created life itself.** As Psalm 119:105 (NIV) reminds us, *"Your word is a lamp for my feet, a light on my path."* Without the guiding light of God's Word, we stumble through life's darkness, making unnecessary mistakes.

The Bible is filled with stories of individuals and nations who experienced blessings when they obeyed God's commands and faced hardships when they disobeyed. Consider the life of King Saul. When God instructed Saul to completely destroy the Amalekites (1 Samuel 15), Saul chose partial obedience; he spared King Agag and kept the best livestock. This act of disobedience cost him the kingdom. **Partial obedience is still disobedience in God's eyes.** Samuel's words to Saul in 1 Samuel 15:22 (NIV) are a timeless reminder: *"To obey is better than sacrifice, and to heed is better than the fat of rams."* This raises a challenging question—are we obeying God fully, or only in the areas that feel convenient?

From a human perspective, God's instructions can sometimes seem illogical or too demanding. He calls us to forgive those who hurt us, to love our enemies, and to trust Him with our finances and future. Yet, obedience is the key that unlocks God's supernatural provision and peace. As Proverbs 3:5-6 (NIV) advises, *"Trust in the Lord with all your heart and lean not on your own understanding; in all your ways submit to him, and he will make your paths straight."* Richard Foster, author of Celebration of Discipline, wrote, "The desperate need today is not for a greater number of intelligent people, or gifted people, but for deep people." Deep people are those who root their lives in obedience to God's truth, even when it contradicts popular culture.

Disobedience, on the other hand, brings unnecessary struggles. Many suffer because they follow their feelings instead of God's commands. They compromise their integrity, hold on to grudges, or rely on human solutions for spiritual problems. James 1:22 (NIV) warns, *"Do not merely listen to the word, and so deceive yourselves. Do what it says."* It's easy to attend church, quote Scripture, and say the right things, but **true** transformation happens when we actively live out God's Word. This brings up a sobering question are we building our lives on the solid rock of obedience or the shifting sand of personal opinion?

For current and future generations, the lesson is clear: **Obedience is not a burden; it is the pathway to blessing.** God's commands are not meant to restrict us but to protect us and lead us into His perfect will. Jesus Himself said in John 14:15 (NIV), *"If you love me, keep my commands."* Obedience is the evidence of genuine love for God. Dwight L. Moody wrote, "The Bible was not given for our information but for our transformation." Moody's words reinforce the truth that **obedience is the natural response of a heart changed by the Word. Future generations must grasp that transformation is not optional for followers of Christ it's expected.**

A CALL TO SURRENDER TO JESUS CHRIST

Surrendering to God is one of the hardest, yet most necessary decisions a person can make. Life's struggles often push people to seek answers in their own strength through personal effort, worldly solutions, or temporary distractions. Yet, **no amount of human strength can heal the deep wounds of the soul.** The world celebrates independence and self-sufficiency, but the Bible teaches that true strength comes through surrender to God. As Proverbs 3:7 (NKJV) says, *"Do not be wise in your own eyes; Fear the Lord and depart from evil."* This raises a crucial question: *Why do so many cling to control when true peace comes from letting go?*

Different people view surrender in different ways. Some see it as weakness, fearing they will lose their identity if they fully submit to God. Others, especially those scarred by disappointment, wonder if God can truly be trusted with their brokenness. Yet, the Bible consistently portrays surrender not as defeat, but as the gateway to divine healing and restoration. *"Casting all your care upon Him, for He cares for you,"* says 1 Peter 5:7 (NKJV). Surrender is not giving up; **it is stepping into God's perfect care.**

Surrender also challenges the illusion of self-sufficiency. Wealth, education, and social status cannot buy inner peace or erase the consequences of sin. Even the strongest and most successful individuals eventually encounter situations they cannot fix, broken relationships, loss, illness, or the weight of guilt. **At that point, surrender becomes the only lifeline.** Jesus offers rest, not just for our bodies but for our weary souls. In Matthew 11:28 (NKJV), He invites, *"Come to Me, all you who labor and are heavy laden, and I will give you rest."* Why continue carrying burdens God is willing to lift?

One of the greatest barriers to surrender is fear of losing control, fear of the unknown, or fear that God will demand too much. Yet, Scripture assures us that God's plans are always for our good. Jeremiah 29:11 (NKJV) declares, *"For I know the thoughts that I think toward you, says the Lord, thoughts of peace and not of evil, to give you a future and a hope."* Hudson Taylor, a missionary to China, described surrendering this way: "All God's giants have been weak men who did great things for God because they reckoned on His being with them." **Taylor points to the paradox of surrender: those who admit their weakness and let God take over become vessels of His strength and glory. True progress begins at the end of self-reliance.**

For current and future generations, it is clear: **Surrender is not a one-time act it is a daily lifestyle of trusting God completely.** In a world obsessed with control and self-reliance, believers must model the beauty of full surrender to Christ. The younger generation needs to see that peace, purpose, and fulfillment flow not from striving, but from resting in God's hands. As 2 Corinthians 6:2 (NKJV) reminds us, *"Behold, now is the accepted time; behold, now is the day of salvation."* Every day is a new invitation to lay down our burdens and walk in the freedom that only surrender can bring.

NOTE THESE

1. True peace and healing come only when we fully surrender to God, not through human strength or worldly solutions.

2. Surrender is not weakness but the doorway to experiencing God's care, guidance, and restoration.

3. We cannot control every aspect of life, but trusting God allows Him to work in ways we could never imagine.

4. Fear of surrender keeps many people bound, but God's plans are always for our good and His glory.

5. Every generation must learn that daily surrender to Jesus leads to a life of true purpose, peace, and fulfillment.

JESUS WILL CARRY YOUR BURDENS

Life often presents overwhelming burdens that can feel impossible to bear alone. **Whether it is financial pressure, sickness, emotional wounds, or guilt from past mistakes, these burdens can weigh heavily on the soul.** Some try to hide their struggles behind a mask of strength, while others openly crumble under the pressure. But is human strength ever enough? The Bible reminds us that we were never meant to carry life's heaviest loads alone. *"Cast all your anxiety on him because he cares for you."* (1 Peter 5:7, NIV). This divine invitation offers hope a reminder that Jesus stands ready to bear our burdens if we would only surrender them into His hands.

From a worldly perspective, independence and self-sufficiency are seen as virtues. Society often teaches that asking for help is a sign of weakness, and vulnerability is avoided at all costs. But **the Kingdom of God operates on a different principle: strength is found in surrender.** The Bible teaches this truth clearly in *2 Corinthians 12:9 (NIV)*: *"But he said to me, 'My grace is sufficient for you, for my power is made perfect in weakness.'"* Why should we pretend to be strong when God invites us to lean on His almighty power? Is it not wiser to let go and allow the Creator to carry what was never meant for us to bear alone?

Many who carry burdens alone end up exhausted and disillusioned. Some chase wealth, thinking financial success will ease their struggles, while others drown their sorrows in harmful habits, hoping to numb the pain. **Yet every human solution eventually fails.** Temporary distractions do not heal deep wounds, and worldly success cannot fill spiritual voids. Jesus offers a far better way. His words in *Matthew 11:28 (NIV)* are a lifeline: *"Come to me, all you who are weary and burdened, and I will give you rest."* True rest is not found in temporary relief but in trusting the One who holds all things together including our broken hearts and weary souls.

The Bible and Christian history are filled with testimonies of those who gave their burdens to God and experienced miraculous transformations. From David's cries for help in the Psalms to Paul's surrender after encountering Jesus on the road to Damascus, God has always responded to surrendered hearts. *Psalm 55:22 (NIV)* echoes this truth: *"Cast your cares on the Lord and he will sustain you; he will never let the righteous be shaken."* No burden is too big, no past is too shameful, and no pain is too deep for God to heal when we trust Him fully.

For current and future generations, the lesson is clear: burdens are inevitable, but carrying them alone is optional. Every generation faces unique struggles, yet the invitation of Jesus remains unchanged: *"Give it to me."* Whether it is the pressure of modern success, the confusion of identity, or the pain of brokenness, the solution is always found in surrendering to Jesus. Will we cling to our pride and continue struggling, or will we accept the loving invitation of the One who promised to carry our burdens and give us rest? The choice, now and always, is ours.

JESUS WILL GIVE YOU REST

In every generation, people long for peace a deep, inner rest that goes beyond momentary comfort. **Yet, many search for peace in the wrong**

places. Some tirelessly pursue wealth, believing that financial success will finally silence their worries. Others seek validation and security in relationships, hoping that human love will fill the void inside. Still, others turn to pleasure, alcohol, or mindless entertainment to numb their fears and anxieties. But does any of this truly satisfy the restless soul? *Jesus Himself answers this question in John 14:27 (NIV): "Peace I leave with you; my peace I give you. I do not give to you as the world gives. Do not let your hearts be troubled and do not be afraid."* This divine peace stands in stark contrast to the fragile peace the world offers.

The world's version of peace is conditional; it depends on favourable circumstances. **When health is good, money is flowing, and relationships are stable, peace seems within reach.** But the moment life takes a downturn, illness strikes, finances crumble, or relationships break, that peace evaporates. How can peace build on unstable foundations ever last? This is why Jesus offers something radically different. His peace is not tied to conditions but to His presence. The peace He gives is unshakable, not because the storms disappear, but because He is Lord over the storm.

True peace is not the absence of trouble, but **the presence of God in the midst of trouble.** This is why the Apostle Paul could write with confidence in *Philippians 4:6-7 (NIV): "Do not be anxious about anything, but in every situation, by prayer and petition, with thanksgiving, present your requests to God. And the peace of God, which transcends all understanding, will guard your hearts and your minds in Christ Jesus."* This peace does not always make logical sense to the world, how can someone facing trials still have inner calm? But this is the supernatural rest that comes when we trust God fully, believing that His hands hold our future.

However, many resist this divine rest because they fear losing control. They believe peace must be achieved through their own efforts working harder, planning more, or securing every outcome. But is this not exhausting? **How much control do we truly have over the future?** Henry Blackaby, author of Experiencing God, wrote, "When you come to the end of yourself, you come to the beginning of God's will." Blackaby speaks directly to the **surrender that must take place** for us to find God's perfect peace. **Only when we let go of our own agendas and plans,** do we open ourselves to God's best for our lives. *Isaiah 26:3 (NIV) reassures us: "You will keep in perfect peace those whose minds are steadfast, because they trust in you."* Trusting God is not passive; it is an active choice to fix our eyes on Him instead of our problems.

For current and future generations, the lesson is clear, rest is not found in possessions, status, or fleeting pleasures. It is found in relationship with Jesus Christ, the Prince of Peace. Every generation will face its own storms, economic uncertainty, relational breakdowns, inner fears but Jesus' invitation remains the same: *"Come to me, all you who are weary and burdened, and I will give you rest."* (Matthew 11:28, NIV). **Will we continue chasing false peace, or will we accept His invitation to find true rest in Him?** This is the defining question that every heart must answer.

TRUST IN JESUS COMPLETELY

Life is unpredictable, filled with uncertainties, challenges, and moments when we feel lost. **Many believe they must have everything figured out before they can trust God, thinking they need to fix their mistakes, understand every situation, or achieve perfection before approaching Him.** However, Jesus never asks us to have all the answers, He simply asks us to trust Him. *Proverbs 3:5-6 (NKJV) reminds us, "Trust in the Lord with all your heart, and lean not on your own understanding; in all your ways acknowledge Him, and He shall direct your paths."* This means that rather than relying on our limited wisdom, we are called to surrender our fears, worries, and plans to God, knowing that He will guide us on the right path.

At times, life does not make sense. **You may be going through a season of hardship, struggling with financial difficulties, battling health issues, facing broken relationships, or carrying a heavy heart.** The enemy whispers lie, making you feel abandoned, hopeless, or unworthy of God's help. But the Bible assures us that God is always faithful. *Jeremiah 29:11 (NKJV) declares, "For I know the thoughts that I think toward you, says the Lord, thoughts of peace and not of evil, to give you a future and a hope."* Even when we do not understand His ways, we can trust that His plans are always for our good. This is a profound reassurance: even in uncertainty, God's purpose for us remains steadfast and filled with hope.

Trusting in Jesus means letting go of the need to control everything. It means walking by faith, even when the road ahead is unclear. *2 Corinthians 5:7 (NKJV) reminds us, "For we walk by faith, not by sight."* When we trust Jesus, He strengthens our hearts, removes our burdens, and leads us into a victorious life. This does not mean we will never face difficulties, but it does mean we will never face them alone. He walks with us, fights for us, and provides for us every step of the way. Our confidence in Christ should not depend on whether we understand our situation but on the unchanging truth that He is with us.

Many hesitate to trust Jesus because they feel unworthy, believing they must fix their lives before coming to Him. **But Jesus calls us just as we are.** *Romans 5:8 (NKJV) assures us, "But God demonstrates His own love toward us, in that while we were still sinners, Christ died for us."* He does not wait for us to be perfect; He welcomes us with open arms, ready to transform our hearts and renew our lives. Just as the prodigal son was welcomed by his father despite his past, Jesus welcomes all who turn to Him in faith. We must reject the lie that we must clean ourselves up before seeking God. Instead, we should trust in His love and grace to do the work of transformation in us.

If you are carrying burdens today, do not hold onto them alone. **Jesus invites you to surrender everything to Him.** *Matthew 11:28 (NKJV) says, "Come to Me, all you who labor and are heavy laden, and I will give you rest."* He is the answer to every worry, every fear, and every struggle. No matter where you are in life, He is calling you to trust Him completely. The question is, *will you keep carrying your burdens, or will you surrender* *them to the One who can truly carry them for you?* Trusting in Jesus is not just a one-time decision; it is a daily act of surrender, allowing Him to lead us into a life of peace, purpose, and victory.

NOTE THESE

1. We do not need to have all the answers before trusting Jesus; He welcomes us as we are.

2. Trusting God means surrendering our worries and allowing Him to guide our path.

3. Even in difficult times, God's plans for us are filled with hope and purpose.

4. True faith means trusting God, not just when life is easy, but even in the darkest moments.

5. When we trust in Jesus completely, we find peace, strength, and rest that the world cannot give.

CHAPTER EIGHT

JESUS IS ABLE TO DELIVER YOU

Life brings moments that feel impossible to overcome, illnesses that doctors cannot cure, financial crises that seem to have no solution, and broken relationships that appear beyond repair. In times like these, **human wisdom and strength often fail**, leaving people feeling hopeless and alone. Yet, the Bible boldly declares that nothing is impossible for God. *Luke 1:37 (NKJV) reminds us, "For with God nothing will be impossible."* This powerful truth invites us to shift our focus from our own limited abilities to the limitless power of God. But do we truly believe this? If God could part the Red Sea (Exodus 14:21) and raise the dead (John 11:43-44), can He not also handle your crisis today? This is the hope that sets faith apart from human logic, it believes in the unseen power of a God who **specializes in impossibilities**.

The world offers many alternatives for deliverance, counseling, medication, financial planning, or motivational self-help strategies. While these can provide temporary relief, **none can bring the deep, soul-level deliverance that only Jesus provides**. The emptiness people feel after exhausting all their options points to a deeper truth: *"I am the Lord, the God of all flesh. Is there anything too hard for Me?" (Jeremiah 32:27, NKJV).* If human strength could solve every problem, why do so many still struggle after trying everything the world offers? It is in our weakest, most desperate moments that God's power shines brightest. True deliverance comes not from self-effort but from surrender.

Faith unlocks the power of God to work in our lives. Hebrews 11:1 (NKJV) defines faith as, *"the substance of things hoped for, the evidence of things not seen."* Faith does not require visible proof it requires trust in God's character and promises. Yet, many Christians struggle with doubt, especially when prayers seem unanswered. Why is it so hard to trust a God who has never failed? Could it be that our view of God has been shaped more by our disappointments than by His Word? A.W. Tozer once wrote, *"What comes into our minds when we think about God is the most important thing about us."* If we truly believe that God is both able and willing to deliver us, our prayers would sound different, our fears would shrink, and our hearts would find rest.

Jesus' invitation in *Matthew 11:28 (NKJV)* says, "Come to Me, all you who labor and are heavy laden, and I will give you rest." This is not a suggestion it is a divine promise. Yet, how often do we refuse this invitation by clinging to our own solutions? What would happen if instead of worrying, we simply came to Jesus, laid down every fear, and said, "I trust You completely"? Deliverance is not found in religious rituals or striving for perfection. It is found in Jesus **the One who welcomes us in our brokenness and transforms our weakness into strength**.

For current and future generations, the lesson is clear: There will always be storms in life, but we do not have to face them alone. The same God who delivered Daniel from the lion's den and Peter from prison is still delivering people today. When everything else fails, Jesus remains faithful. When the world says, "It's over," God says, "I am just getting started." Will you trust Him to deliver you? *"The Lord is my rock and my fortress and my deliverer; My God, my strength, in whom I will trust" (Psalm 18:2, NKJV)*. This is not just ancient truth it is timeless hope for every heart willing to believe.

PUSH THROUGH FAITH

Faith is more than a passive belief it is **active trust expressed through action and perseverance.** Many people pray for breakthroughs but stop pressing forward when challenges arise. They allow fear, doubt, and discouragement to cloud their hope, forgetting that faith that pleases God requires persistence. *Hebrews 11:6 (NKJV) declares, "But without faith it is impossible to please Him, for he who comes to God must believe that He is, and that He is a rewarder of those who diligently seek Him."* This verse teaches that faith is not just about believing in God's existence; it is about actively seeking Him and trusting that He rewards those who refuse to give up. But how often do we give up just before our breakthrough? Can we truly say we trust God if we quit when things get hard?

The story of the woman with the issue of blood in *Mark 5:25-34* is a perfect example of **faith in action.** For twelve years, she suffered, spent all she had on doctors, and only grew worse. According to Jewish law, her condition made her unclean and excluded her from society. Yet, her **faith pushed her beyond social shame, physical weakness, and fear of rejection.** *She said, "If only I may touch His clothes, I shall be made well." (Mark 5:28, NKJV)* Her faith drove her to action she pushed through the crowd and touched Jesus' garment. What would have happened if she had stayed home, believing only in her mind but refusing to step out in faith? Would she have received her healing? This story reminds us that **faith demands courage to act even when circumstances seem impossible.**

Faith without action is **empty and powerless.** James 2:26 (NKJV) emphasizes this truth: *"For as the body without the spirit is dead, so faith without works is dead also."* It is not enough to say we trust God if our actions contradict that trust. Imagine a farmer praying for a great harvest but never planting a single seed. Can he expect a harvest? In the same way, a student who prays for success but refuses to study is not demonstrating true faith. Dietrich Bonhoeffer wrote, "The call of Jesus leads us to the daily decision to follow him." Bonhoeffer highlights that **following Jesus is not a one-time act,** but a **continuous commitment** to live according to His teachings every day, just as **faith is a daily decision** to act in line with our belief.

Many people today are battling issues that seem unmovable financial hardships, health struggles, family conflicts, or deep personal insecurities. It's easy to lose hope when prayers seem unanswered and obstacles seem endless. But just as the woman with the issue of blood refused to be defined by her condition, **we too must refuse to let our struggles define our faith.** *2 Corinthians 5:7 (NKJV) reminds us, "For we walk by faith, not by sight."* Faith chooses to believe God's promise even when the evidence says otherwise. Could it be that your breakthrough is on the other side of your next step of obedience? What if the only thing standing between you and your miracle is the courage to try again?

For both current and future generations, the message is clear: Faith is not passive waiting, it is **active pressing, praying, obeying, and believing until the promise becomes reality.** True faith does not give up when answers are delayed, or obstacles arise. The next time you feel like giving up, remember the woman who touched the hem of Jesus' garment. Let her story remind you that God rewards persistent faith. What breakthrough might be waiting if you choose today to **push through in faith?**

SEIZE THE MOMENT: CALL ON JESUS BEFORE IT'S TOO LATE

Every moment Jesus is near, an opportunity for transformation is within reach. Yet, so many people miss these divine moments because they hesitate, unsure if they qualify for His attention. In Mark 10:46-52, *the blind man Bartimaeus faced the same opportunity, but unlike many, he refused to stay silent.* When Jesus passed by, Bartimaeus cried out boldly: *"Jesus, Son of David, have mercy on me!" (Mark 10:47, NKJV).* Even when the crowd tried to silence him, he shouted louder. This boldness is a lesson for all of us; **when God's presence is near, faith must respond**

with urgency. How many times do we sense God stirring our hearts, but we remain silent out of fear or self-doubt? Could it be that the miracle we seek is only one cry of faith away?

Bartimaeus' story reveals a profound truth: **faith that refuses to be silenced is faith that gets God's attention.** Jesus did not heal him because of his social status, wealth, or religious qualifications. *He healed him because of his persistent, unwavering faith.* Bartimaeus understood that **faith is not passive; it calls, it cries, and it reaches.** James 4:8 (NKJV) affirms this: *"Draw near to God and He will draw near to you."* This verse highlights a divine principle: **God responds to those who take steps toward Him.** But how often do people hesitate, waiting for a perfect moment or for God to move first? In reality, **faith takes the first step.** As evangelist Smith Wigglesworth once said, *"God will pass over a million people to get to the one who dares to believe."*

Some people remain silent because they feel unworthy. They think their problems are too small for God, or their sins are too great to be forgiven. But the Bible clearly teaches that *Jesus came to seek and save the lost (Luke 19:10, NKJV)*; no one is too far gone for His mercy. Others hesitate because they fear the opinions of people around them. Bartimaeus teaches us that **the crowd's opinion does not decide your miracle your faith does.** In Matthew 7:7 (NKJV), Jesus Himself says: *"Ask, and it will be given to you; seek, and you will find; knock, and it will be opened to you."* If Bartimaeus had let fear or shame silence him, he would have missed his healing. What miracle could be waiting if we stopped fearing people and started crying out to Jesus with boldness?

The story also shows us that **opportunities with Jesus are often time-sensitive.** Jesus was passing by He wasn't planning to stop until Bartimaeus' cry halted Him. This reminds us that some divine moments will never come again if we let them slip by. *Proverbs 8:17 (NKJV) says, "I love those who love me, and those who seek me diligently will find me."* This is a call to **spiritual urgency.** Imagine standing at the roadside, needing help, and a rescue vehicle passes would you hesitate to call out? The same applies to our spiritual lives. When Jesus is near, silence is costly. **Opportunities in God's presence are too valuable to waste.**

For today's generation and the future, the lesson is clear: When Jesus is near, respond boldly. No fear, failure, or public opinion should silence your cry for mercy. Charles Spurgeon said, "Faith is the open hand that receives from God." Faith calls out even when the crowd discourages it. Faith steps forward even when shame whispers, "Stay back." Future generations must learn that **the cry of faith can change destiny.** No one who sincerely seeks Jesus will be ignored. As *Jeremiah 29:13 (NKJV)* assures: *"And you will seek Me and find Me, when you search for Me with all your heart."* **Let every heart know this truth: Jesus is passing by, and now is the time to cry out.** Will you stay silent, or will you reach for your miracle?

NOTE THESE

1. Faith must be bold and persistent, refusing to be silenced by fear, doubt, or public opinion.

2. Opportunities with Jesus are time-sensitive, when He is near, we must act immediately.

3. No one is too unworthy or too broken to receive mercy from Jesus when they call on Him sincerely.

4. The opinions of others should never stop us from seeking our miracle through faith.

5. God responds to those who seek Him wholeheartedly, and He never ignores a sincere cry for help.

BREAK FREE FROM EVERY STRONGHOLD

In life, many people walk around carrying invisible chains and strongholds that silently dictate their thoughts, decisions, and destinies. These strongholds come in many forms: fear, addiction, shame, sickness, or generational curses. Some are born from personal failures, while others are inherited burdens passed down through families. Yet, **the glorious truth is this no stronghold is stronger than the power of Jesus Christ.** As *Isaiah 61:1 (NKJV)* proclaims, *"The Spirit of the Lord GOD is upon Me because the LORD has anointed Me to preach good tidings to the poor; He has sent Me to heal the brokenhearted, to proclaim liberty to the captives, and the opening of the prison to those who are bound."* Jesus did not come to offer temporary relief He came to set captives **completely free.** So why do many believers still live bound? Is it possible that fear, doubt, or even comfort in familiar struggles keeps them from stepping into true freedom?

Jesus desires victory for every person, but walking in freedom requires surrender. Some people struggle because they fight their battles alone, forgetting that **deliverance is a divine partnership.** While human effort has its limits, God's power knows no bounds. When fear grips the heart and anxiety takes over the mind, we must remember that *2 Timothy 1:7 (NKJV)* declares, *"For God has not given us a spirit of fear, but of power and of love and of a sound mind."* Why fear when the One who holds all power has called you His own? Watchman Nee affirmed, "Deliverance from sin is not by struggling, but by letting go and letting Christ take over." Nee emphasizes that **victory over sin comes through surrender,** not sheer effort. When believers yield control, **Christ empowers them** to overcome temptation and walk in freedom.

Sin remains one of the strongest chains, one that no human's strength can break. Many have tried to reform themselves through self-discipline, positive thinking, or sheer willpower. Yet, without Jesus, these efforts are like washing a stained cloth with dirty water. **Only the blood of Jesus can cleanse the soul.** As *1 John 1:9 (NKJV)* assures us, *"If we confess our sins, He is faithful and just to forgive us our sins and to cleanse us from all unrighteousness."* God's forgiveness is not partial it is complete, erasing guilt and restoring peace. Even when sin whispers, "You are too far gone," God's mercy responds, "Come home."

Beyond personal struggles, **spiritual oppression is another weapon the enemy uses to enslave souls.** Many find themselves in cycles of affliction, physical illnesses with no medical explanation, unrelenting failures, or a deep sense of hopelessness. In such moments, it is easy to believe the lie that freedom is out of reach. But Jesus has already defeated the enemy! As *Luke 10:19 (NKJV)* boldly declares, *"Behold, I give you the authority to trample on serpents and scorpions, and over all the power of the enemy, and nothing shall by any means hurt you."* So why do many still live afraid? Could it be that they have forgotten the authority they carry in Christ? Spiritual battles are real, but **victory belongs to those who fight with God's Word, prayer, and unwavering faith.**

Finally, **the invitation to freedom stands open to all,** but it requires action. Jesus has already paid the price for every person to walk free, yet not all choose to step out of the prison cell. As *John 8:36 (NKJV)* declares, *"Therefore if the Son makes you free, you shall be free indeed."* True freedom is not just the absence of struggle; it is the presence of divine peace, purpose, and power. Why settle for chains when Jesus offers keys? As future generations rise, they must be taught that **freedom is a gift, but it must be embraced.** Today's believers must pass down not just faith, but the unshakable truth that **strongholds can and will break when surrendered to Jesus.** After all, **why remain a prisoner when you were born to be free?**

JESUS BREAKS EVERY CURSE AND BARRIER

In biblical times, leprosy was a disease that went beyond the physical. It represented rejection, shame, and a painful separation from society. Those affected were seen as outcasts, unworthy of love or acceptance. Today, **many people carry invisible "leprosy" the shame and pain of generational curses, broken homes, financial struggles, and spiritual barriers that seem impossible to overcome.** But here is the truth: **Jesus specializes in breaking every curse and barrier.** As *Galatians 3:13 (NKJV)* boldly declares, *"Christ has redeemed us from the curse of the law, having become a curse for us (for it is written, 'Cursed is everyone who hangs on* *a tree')."* If Jesus has already carried the curse for us, why should we continue to live under its weight? Is it possible that some have become so used to bondage that they no longer believe freedom is possible?

Generational curses are real, but **they are not final.** Some families experience repeated patterns of poverty, disease, addiction, and failure, passing from one generation to the next like an unwanted inheritance. Many accept this as their destiny, thinking it is "just the way life is." But this mindset contradicts the victory Jesus secured on the cross. *Isaiah 54:17 (NKJV)* assures us, *"No weapon formed against you shall prosper, and every tongue which rises against you in judgment you shall condemn."* **Every curse can be broken by the authority of God's Word and the power of faith.** Beth Moore said, "God is always doing 10,000 things in your life, and you may be aware of three of them." So why settle for defeat when divine freedom is already promised? This quote challenges believers not to **limit their expectations** of what God can do. He is **constantly at work,** even when we can't see it, just as He's always been throughout Scripture.

God's desire for His children is not just survival but complete restoration. No matter how deep the wounds, how long the suffering, or how impossible the situation may seem, God is able to restore all that has been lost. *Joel 2:25 (NKJV)* offers this powerful promise: *"So I will restore to you the years that the swarming locust has eaten."* Can you imagine God returning years of brokenness and transforming them into testimonies of His faithfulness? He does not simply remove the curse; He replaces it with blessing, healing, and purpose. The question is **will you trust God enough to break the cycle, or will you choose to stay in familiar chains?**

Even when the past whispers that change is impossible, **God's Word speaks a better truth.** His promises carry more authority than family history, cultural beliefs, or personal failures. **Jesus not only broke the curse but gave His followers the authority to enforce their freedom.** Through prayer, faith, and obedience to God's Word, **barriers crumble, curses are reversed, and new legacies are created.** *2 Corinthians 5:17*

(NKJV) confirms this: *"Therefore, if anyone is in Christ, he is a new creation; old things have passed away; behold, all things have become new."* Your past does not have to dictate your future; **in Christ, you are free to write a new story.**

For current and future generations, **the greatest lesson is this: no curse is greater than the cross, and no barrier is stronger than God's promises.** Families must teach their children not to accept generational pain as destiny but to **stand on God's Word and walk in the victory Jesus secured.** What legacy will you leave behind, a chain of curses or a testimony of deliverance? As believers, **we are called not only to break free but to break others free** by sharing the hope we have in Christ. After all, **why pass down chains when we can pass down blessings?**

HE BREAKS EVERY CURSE AND BARRIER

In biblical times, leprosy was a disease that went beyond the physical. It represented rejection, shame, and a painful separation from society. Those affected were seen as outcasts, unworthy of love or acceptance. Today, **many people carry invisible "leprosy" the shame and pain of generational curses, broken homes, financial struggles, and spiritual barriers that seem impossible to overcome.** But here is the truth: **Jesus specializes in breaking every curse and barrier.** As *Galatians 3:13 (NKJV)* boldly declares, *"Christ has redeemed us from the curse of the law, having become a curse for us (for it is written, 'Cursed is everyone who hangs on a tree')."* If Jesus has already carried the curse for us, why should we continue to live under its weight? Is it possible that some have become so used to bondage that they no longer believe freedom is possible?

Generational curses are real, but **they are not final.** Some families experience repeated patterns of poverty, disease, addiction, and failure, passing from one generation to the next like an unwanted inheritance. Many accept this as their destiny, thinking it is "just the way life is." But this mindset contradicts the victory Jesus secured on the cross. *Isaiah 54:17 (NKJV)* assures us, *"No weapon formed against you shall prosper, and every tongue which rises against you in judgment you shall condemn."* **Every curse can be broken by the authority of God's Word and the power of faith. As Henry Blackaby, author of *Experiencing God* once said, *"Will God ever ask you to do something you are not able to do? The answer is yes, all the time! It must be that way, for God's glory and kingdom. If we function according to our ability alone, we get the glory; if we function according to the power of the Spirit within us, God gets the glory."* So why settle for defeat when divine freedom is already promised?

God's desire for His children is not just survival but complete restoration. No matter how deep the wounds, how long the suffering, or how impossible the situation may seem, God is able to restore all that has been lost. *Joel 2:25 (NKJV)* offers this powerful promise: *"So I will restore to you the years that the swarming locust has eaten."* Can you imagine God returning years of brokenness and transforming them into testimonies of His faithfulness? He does not simply remove the curse; He replaces it with blessing, healing, and purpose. The question is **will you trust God enough to break the cycle, or will you choose to stay in familiar chains?**

Even when the past whispers that change is impossible, **God's Word speaks a better truth.** His promises carry more authority than family history, cultural beliefs, or personal failures. **Jesus not only broke the curse but gave His followers the authority to enforce their freedom.** Through prayer, faith, and obedience to God's Word, **barriers crumble, curses are reversed, and new legacies are created.** *2 Corinthians 5:17 (NKJV)* confirms this: *"Therefore, if anyone is in Christ, he is a new creation; old things have passed away; behold, all things have become new."* Your past does not have to dictate your future; **in Christ, you are free to write a new story.**

For current and future generations, **the greatest lesson is this: no curse is greater than the cross, and no barrier is stronger than God's promises.** Families must teach their children not to accept generational pain as destiny, but to **stand on God's Word and walk in the victory Jesus secured.** What legacy will you leave behind, a chain of curses or a testimony of deliverance? As believers, **we are called not only to break**

free but to break others free by sharing the hope we have in Christ. After all, **why pass down chains when we can pass down blessings?**

NOTE THESE

1. No curse or generational barrier is greater than the power of Jesus' sacrifice on the cross.

2. Faith in God's Word gives believers the authority to break free from every stronghold and curse.

3. God's desire is not just to free us from bondage, but to restore all that has been lost.

4. Every believer has the responsibility to reject generational defeat and embrace God's promises for a new legacy.

5. Freedom in Christ is not just personal; it is meant to be passed down to future generations.

9

CHAPTER NINE

DON'T SIT BACK AND WATCH – TAKE ACTION

Many individuals witness the struggles in their lives, families, and communities but **choose to do nothing**, believing that suffering is simply their destiny. This mindset of passive acceptance is dangerous because it gives room for darkness to thrive unchecked. The Bible declares in *Hosea 4:6 (NIV)*: *"my people are destroyed from lack of knowledge."* What knowledge do they lack? The knowledge that God has given them the authority to confront and overcome these struggles. How many people today are bound, not because God cannot save them, but because they refuse to rise and act in faith? As Watchman Nee noted, "Our prayers lay the track down on which God's power can come." Prayer, combined with action, invites heaven into earthly situations.

The devil, who is described in *John 10:10 (NIV)* as *"The thief comes only to steal and kill and destroy,"* thrives where there is ignorance and passivity. **Many hardships people face are not ordinary life challenges, but spiritual battles requiring spiritual confrontation.** Yet, the enemy is not unstoppable *James 4:7 (NIV)* reminds us: *"Resist the devil, and he will flee from you."* The key word here is **resist**; resistance requires intentional action, not passive endurance. Why should the enemy continue to have authority over a family, marriage, or business when God has given believers the power to fight back through prayer, obedience, and bold faith?

Faith, as emphasized in *James 2:26 (NIV)*, *"As the body without the spirit is dead, so faith without deeds is dead,"* demands movement, not silence. Many believers pray for breakthrough but are unwilling to change unhealthy habits, step out in faith, or obey divine instructions. Can one truly claim to have faith while refusing to act? This balance between faith and action is crucial. Prayer invites God's power, but obedience releases it into practical situations.

Taking action does not mean relying on human strength alone, but aligning with divine promises through active faith. If a family struggles with generational poverty, someone must rise to **reject that cycle** by embracing God's principles of stewardship, generosity, and diligence. *2 Chronicles 7:14 (NIV)* states: *"If my people, who are called by my name, will humble themselves and pray and seek my face and turn from their wicked ways, then I will hear from heaven, and I will forgive their sin and will heal their land."* Notice the action verbs humble, pray, seek, and turn. These are intentional steps of faith that invite God's intervention. Why should the next generation inherit the same struggles if today's generation can break the cycle?

The choice to act or remain passive is a matter of legacy. Psalm 34:17 (NIV) assures us: *"The righteous cry out, and the Lord hears them; he delivers them from all their troubles."* Deliverance is not promised to those who sit back silently but to those who cry out in faith. Leonard Ravenhill said, "The only reason we don't have revival is because we are willing to live without it." This truth applies to personal and family breakthroughs as well. **If we settle for suffering, suffering will continue; if we act in faith, God will move.** For today's generation and those to come, the lesson is clear: **Passivity prolongs bondage, but faith-filled action releases God's power.**

NOTE THESE

1. Ignoring spiritual struggles allows them to grow stronger, affecting future generations.

2. Faith without action will not produce lasting change.

3. The enemy thrives where there is silence and ignorance, but he flees where there is resistance.

4. Prayer must be followed by steps of faith and obedience to God's Word.

5. Every generation must choose whether to pass on faith or generational struggles to their children.

GOD HAS THE POWER TO SILENCE THE DEVIL

The enemy will continue to attack, **but only for as long as believers allow him** to operate unchecked. Many Christians live under unnecessary fear, believing that the devil has limitless power over their lives. This is a dangerous misunderstanding of spiritual authority. *Luke 10:19 (NIV)* declares: *"I have given you authority to trample on snakes and scorpions and to overcome all the power of the enemy; nothing will harm you."* This verse reveals a profound truth — believers have not only protection but power. So why do so many live in fear? Is it because they forget who they are in Christ? As the great preacher Smith Wigglesworth once said, "Great faith is the product of great fights. Great testimonies are the outcome of great tests. Great triumphs can only come out of great trials."

The enemy thrives where there is **ignorance of divine authority**. When people fail to realize who they are in Christ, they become easy prey for the devil's schemes. However, the moment a believer stands on God's promises, **everything changes**. The Bible gives countless examples of individuals delivered from oppression because they encountered the power of God. One of the most striking is the story of the man possessed by a legion of demons in Mark 5. This man's life was completely out of control, living among tombs, violent, and feared by all. Yet, *Mark 5:15 (NIV)* says: *"When they came to Jesus, they saw the man who had been possessed by the legion of demons, sitting there, dressed and in his right mind; and they were afraid."* If Jesus could silence an entire legion of demons with a word, what can He do in your life today?

No stronghold is too powerful for God's deliverance. This is a foundational truth many forget when faced with prolonged battles. Sometimes sickness, fear, or generational bondage seems so deeply rooted that freedom feels impossible. Yet, *1 John 4:4 (NIV)* reminds us: *"You, dear children, are from God and have overcome them, because the one who is in you is greater than the one who is in the world."* If the Spirit of God dwells within you, how can any force of darkness permanently prevail? Neil T. Anderson, author of The Bondage Breaker once wrote, "The only power Satan has over you is the power of a lie. And when you expose the lie, his power is broken." Anderson reminds us that Satan operates through **deception**, not actual authority over a child of God.

Deliverance is not only for those with extreme demonic oppression – **it is for anyone held captive by fear, addiction, sickness, or sin**. Jesus came not just to forgive sins but to destroy the works of the devil. *1 John 3:8 (NIV)* states: *"The reason the Son of God appeared was to destroy the devil's work."* This is why believers cannot remain passive in the face of spiritual attacks. They must rise in faith, apply the Word, and take authority in Jesus' name. As *Isaiah 54:17 (NIV)* declares: *"No weapon forged against you will prevail, and you will refute every tongue that accuses you."* The enemy can only win when believers surrender their authority through fear or neglect.

The lesson for both **current and future generations** is clear authority **unused is authority wasted**. Christians must teach their children, families, and communities how to walk in spiritual authority. Passive Christianity leaves room for the enemy to build strongholds. But when believers rise in faith, pray with authority, and apply God's Word, the devil has no option but to retreat. As Leonard Ravenhill said, "The greatest tragedy is a prayerless Christian." The time for silence and fear is over the time to walk boldly in victory is now.

NOTE THESE

1. Ignorance of spiritual authority keeps people in unnecessary bondage.
2. God has given every believer the power to overcome all the works of the enemy.
3. Deliverance is available to anyone who stands in faith and takes authority in Jesus' name.
4. The devil can only thrive where fear, passivity, and silence exist.
5. Spiritual authority must be taught, practiced, and passed on to future generations.

THESE ARE NOT JUST STORIES – THEY ARE REAL

Too many people, even within the church, have reduced the Bible to a collection of ancient tales, **treating it like a history textbook rather than the living, breathing Word of God.** They read about Moses parting the Red Sea, Elijah calling down fire from heaven, and Jesus walking on water, yet they struggle to believe these events actually happened, much less that they could happen again. However, *2 Timothy 3:16 (NIV)* reminds us: *"All Scripture is God-breathed and is useful for teaching, rebuking, correcting and training in righteousness."* If the Bible is divinely inspired, how can any part of it be treated as mere fiction? Can a God who created the universe lie? Charles Spurgeon once said, *"A Bible that's falling apart usually belongs to someone who isn't."* This highlights the power of Scripture when it is embraced as truth rather than myth.

Every miracle in the Bible is not just a story; **it is a divine testimony** of God's power and love in action. These miracles are not locked in the pages of ancient history but are living proof of what God can still do today. *Hebrews 13:8 (NIV)* declares: *"Jesus Christ is the same yesterday and today and forever."* If God has not changed, why should His power?

If He opened blind eyes and raised the dead before, what stops Him from doing it now? These miracles were not given just to amaze people; they were recorded so future generations could know that God's power is timeless. As A.W. Tozer said, "Anything God has ever done, He can do now. Anything God has ever done anywhere, He can do here."

One reason many doubt the reality of biblical miracles is because they have never experienced one personally. But does the absence of personal experience negate truth? **Faith is the key that unlocks the miraculous.** Jesus Himself said in *Mark 9:23 (NIV)*: *"Everything is possible for one who believes."* If belief activates God's power, could unbelief be the very thing that limits His work in our lives? This is why testimonies matter they are modern evidence of ancient truths. When people share how God healed them, provided miraculously, or intervened supernaturally, they show that the God of Scripture is still actively working today.

The enemy's greatest weapon is doubt, convincing people that God is no longer a God of miracles. If he can make believers view the Bible as outdated, he can strip them of the faith necessary to experience divine power. Yet, *Jeremiah 32:27 (NIV)* asks: *"I am the Lord, the God of all mankind. Is anything too hard for me?"* What could possibly limit an all-powerful God? Corrie ten Boom, who witnessed God's miraculous protection during the Holocaust, once said, *"There is no pit so deep, that God's love is not deeper still."* This same God who moved mountains in the Bible is still moving mountains today, if only His people would believe.

For this generation and the next, **the challenge is clear: see the Bible as reality, not mythology**. When Scripture is treated as truth, faith rises, and miracles follow. Parents must teach their children that these stories are not fairy tales, but real-life accounts of God's glory. Churches must preach with conviction that miracles are not ancient history, but present-day possibilities. What God did before, He can do again and even greater (John 14:12). **It is time to read the Bible with expectation, pray with boldness, and believe with unwavering faith.** These are not just stories, **they are living testimonies of the God who still reigns today.**

FAITH OVER EXPECTATIONS

In life, it is natural to have expectations, plans for how things should unfold, dreams of when breakthroughs should happen, and visions of how success should look. However, **the danger comes when these human expectations are placed above faith in God's perfect will.** When things do not go as expected, frustration and disappointment creep in. This is why *Isaiah 55:8-9 (NIV)* reminds us: *"For my thoughts are not your thoughts, neither are your ways my ways," declares the LORD. "As the heavens are higher than the earth, so are my ways higher than your ways and my thoughts than your thoughts."* If God's thoughts are higher, why should we expect Him to fit into the small box of our expectations? Could it be that unmet expectations are often divine redirections?

Faith does not depend on visible outcomes; **faith trusts even when logic fails.** Abraham's life is a perfect example, God promised him a child at a time when his body was too old to produce one. Any human expectation would have called that promise impossible. Yet, *Romans 4:20-21 (NIV)* declares: *"Yet he did not waver through unbelief regarding the promise of God, but was strengthened in his faith and gave glory to God, being fully persuaded that God had power to do what he had promised."* Abraham's faith was not in a timeline or a method, but in the character and power of God. What would happen if we stopped placing deadlines on God and started placing trust in His timing?

When prayers seem to go unanswered, faith steps in to remind us that God is never inactive. Closed doors are not denials, but often redirections toward something better. Faith teaches us that every delay has a purpose, every detour holds a lesson, and every disappointment can lead to divine appointment. *Hebrews 11:1 (NIV)* says: *"Now faith is confidence in what we hope for and assurance about what we do not see."* This kind of faith looks past current circumstances and trusts in the unseen hand of God. Can faith still thrive when the future is uncertain?

Human expectations are shaped by personal desires, cultural pressures, and limited understanding. But **faith surrenders control and allows**

God to work in ways far beyond imagination. When Martha expected Jesus to heal Lazarus before death, her limited expectation blinded her to the greater miracle of resurrection. Similarly, we often expect God to act within our comfort zone, forgetting that His ways exceed our logic. Ephesians 3:20 (NIV) declares: *"Now to him who is able to do immeasurably more than all we ask or imagine, according to his power that is at work within us."* What if the delay you are frustrated with is actually preparing you for something greater than you could have expected?

For this generation and the ones to come, **the challenge is to embrace faith over expectations.** This means holding dreams lightly and holding God's hand tightly. It means praying with boldness but trusting with humility. As Oswald Chambers said, "Faith never knows where it is being led, but it loves and knows the One who is leading." When expectations fall apart, faith holds firm. **Choose faith over expectations, and you will witness God writing a story greater than anything you could have scripted yourself.**

HUMAN EXPECTATIONS AND GOD'S DIVINE WAYS

It is natural for people to approach God with their own ideas of how He should act. **We often expect God to work according to our personal timelines and limited logic, forgetting that His wisdom surpasses human understanding.** This mindset creates frustration when answers do not come in the expected way. But God is not bound by human frameworks; His ways are higher and His methods are far beyond human imagination. *Isaiah 55:8-9 (NIV)* declares: *"For my thoughts are not your thoughts, neither are your ways my ways," declares the* LORD*. "As the heavens are higher than the earth, so are my ways higher than your ways and my thoughts than your thoughts."* Does it make sense to demand that the Creator of the universe fit into human plans? Can limited human understanding truly dictate how an infinite God should work?

One of the greatest hindrances to experiencing God's miracles is rigid expectation. Many people imagine God's intervention must come through dramatic signs, thunderous voices, or extraordinary encounters.

Yet, God often works through simple, unexpected moments, through a whisper, a gentle nudge, or a quiet instruction. In 2 Kings 5, Naaman almost missed his healing because he expected the prophet Elisha to call on God with grand gestures. Instead, Elisha told him to simply wash in the Jordan River. *This teaches us that divine answers often arrive in humble forms.* As Henri Nouwen, in Mere Christianity, "We are not what we do... we are not what we have, we are not what other people say about us. We are the beloved daughters and sons of God." Faith begins when we stop dictating and start surrendering.

The Bible repeatedly warns against relying too heavily on human reasoning. *Proverbs 3:5-6 (*NIV*)* instructs: *"Trust in the LORD with all your heart and lean not on your own understanding; in all your ways submit to him, and he will make your paths straight."* **Faith does not demand answers; faith trusts even when answers are unclear.** Human wisdom sees obstacles; divine wisdom sees opportunities. What if the answer to your prayer has already arrived, but because it did not match your expectation, you failed to recognize it? Oswald Chambers puts it this way: "Faith never knows where it is being led, but it loves and knows the One who is leading."

Another critical truth is that **God often uses the 'foolish' things to display His greatest power.** What appears insignificant or strange to human eyes is often God's chosen path. *1 Corinthians 1:27 (*NIV*)* confirms this: *"But God chose the foolish things of the world to shame the wise; God chose the weak things of the world to shame the strong."* This challenges every believer to abandon the need to 'understand' everything and instead embrace a childlike faith. When Jesus healed with a word, spat in mud to open blind eyes, or simply said, "Go, your faith has healed you," it often defied logic, yet miracles happened. **Would you miss your miracle because the method feels too simple?**

For this generation and those to come, the greatest lesson is this: **expect God to move, but do not dictate how.** Trusting God means releasing the need for control and embracing His mysterious, perfect ways.

Every delay, every unusual instruction, and every unexpected twist can be part of His greater purpose. As Philip Yancey said, "Grace means there is nothing we can do to make God love us more… and nothing we can do to make God love us less." Instead of resisting His ways, embrace them with faith and humility, knowing that His divine plan always exceeds human expectation. **When we let go of our plans, we make room for His miracles.**

FAITH IS THE KEY TO MIRACLES

Many believers long to experience miracles but struggle to receive them because they overcomplicate what God has made beautifully simple. In a world where people are conditioned to believe that extraordinary results require extraordinary effort, the simplicity of faith can feel too easy to be true. Yet, *Hebrews 11:6 (NIV)* clearly states: *"And without faith it is impossible to please God, because anyone who comes to him must believe that he exists and that he rewards those who earnestly seek him."* Is it possible that many miss their miracles not because God is unwilling, but because they are too busy trying to earn what can only be received by faith? Andrew Murray said, "Faith expects from God what is beyond all expectation."

Often, God's miracles come wrapped in simple instructions, ones that require trust more than understanding. Human nature tends to crave dramatic signs and complex processes, yet God consistently reveals His power through humble acts of faith and obedience. When Jesus healed the blind man, He simply said, *"Go, wash in the Pool of Siloam"* (John 9:7, NIV). No long prayer, no complicated ritual just faith-filled obedience. *John 3:16 (NIV)* declares: *"For God so loved the world that he gave his one and only Son, that whoever believes in him shall not perish but have eternal life."* If the greatest miracle, salvation, comes through something as simple as believing, why do we expect other miracles to be more complicated? Joni Eareckson Tada captured this beautifully when he said, "God allows what he hates to accomplish what he loves."

Faith is impossible without humility. Pride often blocks the flow of God's power because pride insists on its own way, demanding that God work according to human terms and timelines. Yet, *Proverbs 3:5-6 (NIV)* reminds us: *"Trust in the Lord with all your heart and lean not on your own understanding; in all your ways submit to him, and he will make your paths straight."* How often do people miss their miracle simply because they are unwilling to surrender their pride? John Wesley affirmed, "Give me 100 preachers who fear nothing but sin, and desire nothing but God, and I care not a straw whether they be clergy or laymen. Such alone will shake the gates of hell and set up the kingdom of heaven on earth." This powerful quote by Wesley reflects how surrendering to God, abandoning self-reliance, and completely depending on Him can bring powerful transformation, similar to the concept of miracles taking place when self-sufficiency ends.

Faith is more than belief, it is active obedience to God's Word. Jesus' invitations are not complex theological puzzles, but simple calls to trust and follow. *"Come to me, all who are weary, and I will give you rest." (Matthew 11:28, NIV). "Ask and you will receive." (Matthew 7:7, NIV). "Whoever believes in me, as Scripture has said, rivers of living water will flow from within them." (John 7:38, NIV).* These are not riddles to decode, but invitations to respond with simple, childlike faith. **When faith moves, miracles follow.** Do we overthink God's promises because they seem too simple to be true? Or could it be that true faith requires the courage to believe without demanding all the details first?

Ultimately, **miracles are not earned through human effort; they are received through faith.** The kingdom of God does not operate like the world in God's economy, **faith is the currency that unlocks heaven's storehouse.** No matter how impossible the situation may seem, faith opens the door to healing, provision, and restoration. The only question is are you willing to believe even when logic says it's impossible? *Mark 9:23 (NIV)* affirms: *"Everything is possible for one who believes."* Miracles are not distant or rare, they are waiting on the other side of faith.

NOTE THESE

1. Miracles are received through simple faith, not through complicated efforts or rituals.
2. God often works through humble obedience to His Word, even when His instructions seem too simple.
3. Pride blocks miracles, but humility and surrender open the door to God's power.
4. Faith is not just believing God exists but trusting His promises and acting on them.
5. God's miracles are still available today to those who are willing to believe, obey, and trust in His perfect ways.

DON'T REJECT GOD BECAUSE OF HUMAN LOGIC

Many people miss out on the wonders of God because they try to fit Him into the small box of human understanding. They want God to act in ways that align with their logic and reasoning, but **God is not confined to human wisdom.** *Isaiah 55:8-9 (NIV) declares: "For my thoughts are not your thoughts, neither are your ways my ways," declares the Lord. "As the heavens are higher than the earth, so are my ways higher than your ways and my thoughts than your thoughts."* If God's ways are higher than ours, why should we expect Him to always make sense to our limited minds? Isn't it possible that God, who created the universe, could work in ways we cannot fully grasp? As J.I. Packer affirmed, "If we are to bring God into our thinking, we must begin by acknowledging that His ways are not our ways, His thoughts are higher than ours. We are to humbly accept the mystery of His greatness, not try to reduce it to what we can understand." When we reduce God to the level of our logic, we are no longer worshipping the true God, but a version we have created to fit our comfort.

Some people doubt the power of prayer because they cannot explain how it works. They choose to rely on their own strength rather than trusting in God's invisible hand. But *James 5:16 (NIV) reminds us: "The prayer of a righteous person is powerful and effective."* If prayer works beyond human logic, why do we insist on understanding it thoroughly before we believe? Should a child refuse to eat because they don't understand how digestion works? In the same way, believers must trust that prayer is effective because God has declared it so, not because they can explain every step. As Oswald Chambers wrote, "Prayer does not fit us for the greater work; prayer is the greater work." To reject prayer because of human logic is to reject one of the most powerful tools God has given to His people.

The message of salvation itself defies human logic. Can eternal life truly come from simply believing in Jesus and confessing Him as Lord? Human reasoning might demand more work, rituals, and intellectual understanding, but *Romans 10:9 (NIV) states: "If you declare with your mouth, 'Jesus is Lord,' and believe in your heart that God raised him from the dead, you will be saved."* Isn't it amazing that something so profound can be so simple? Yet, some reject this simplicity, believing it is too easy to be true. N.T. Wright observed, "The gospel is not primarily about what we do for God, but what God has done for us, and what that means for our present and our future." Salvation is not a formula to be solved, but a gift to be received by faith. When human logic demands a complex explanation, faith simply says, "I believe."

Even the way God works miracles often offends human logic. In *John 9:6-7 (NIV)*, Jesus healed a blind man by making mud with His saliva and telling him to wash in a specific pool. To human reasoning, this makes no sense but to God, it was the perfect method to demonstrate both healing and obedience. How often do we miss our miracle because we argue with God's methods? *1 Corinthians 1:27 (NIV) teaches: "But God chose the foolish things of the world to shame the wise; God chose the weak things of the world to shame the strong."* Miracles happen not when we understand every step, but when we trust God enough to obey, even when the method seems foolish. As Andrew Murray once wrote, "Faith expects from God what is beyond all expectation." **God** is not limited by human logic; He is only limited by our unwillingness to trust Him. When we let go of the need to understand everything and choose instead to believe, we open the door for God to do the impossible in our lives.

NOTE THESE

1. God's ways are far beyond human understanding, so trusting Him requires faith, not logic.
2. Prayer is powerful even when we cannot fully explain how it works.
3. Salvation is a gift received by simple faith, not by complicated reasoning.
4. God's miracles often come through unexpected methods, requiring obedience over understanding.
5. Limiting God to human logic blocks the supernatural work He wants to do in our lives.

10

CHAPTER TEN

HE KNOWS THE WAY

Many people struggle to trust God because they expect Him to move in ways that fit their imagination. They look for dramatic miracles, audible voices, or supernatural signs before they are willing to believe. But **faith does not depend on visible proof it requires confidence in God's character and His promises.** As Hebrews 11:1 (NIV) says, *"Now faith is confidence in what we hope for and assurance about what we do not see."* This verse reveals a key truth: **faith means believing before seeing**, not the other way around. What if God's plan for you is already unfolding quietly, without the fireworks you expected? Would you still trust Him?

Some people postpone surrendering their lives to God because they are waiting for the "perfect moment." They assume they need to fix their brokenness, overcome their struggles, or become "worthy" before God will accept them. Yet, this mindset is far from biblical truth. Romans 5:8 (NIV) clearly states, *"But God demonstrates his own love for us in this: While we were still sinners, Christ died for us."* God meets people right where they are, in their weakness and imperfection. **Why wait for perfection when God's love is already reaching out to you?** True faith begins when we stop trying to qualify ourselves and start trusting His grace.

Others want a spectacular encounter with God before they believe. They desire a heavenly vision, an angelic visitation, or a dramatic sign. But God often moves in subtle, quiet ways through gentle nudges, whispers in prayer, or simple moments of peace. In 1 Kings 19:11-12 (NIV), the prophet Elijah experienced this truth: *"The Lord was not in the wind… the earthquake… or the fire. And after the fire came a gentle whisper."* Could it be that **God is already speaking, but in ways quieter than you expected?** Oswald Chambers wrote, "The great thing about faith in God is that it keeps a man undisturbed in the midst of disturbance." Faith is not waiting for fireworks it is recognizing God even in stillness.

Faith is not just a feeling; it demands action. James 2:26 (NIV) states, *"As the body without the spirit is dead, so faith without deeds is dead."* Many people miss their blessings because they hesitate to obey when God's instructions seem too simple or confusing. Consider the blind man in John 9:6-7 (NIV), who was healed only after obeying Jesus' unusual command to wash in the Pool of Siloam. What if your miracle is just one simple step of obedience away? **Faith is not passive it moves, acts, and obeys, even when the path seems unclear.** As A.W. Tozer wrote, *"Faith is the gaze of a soul upon a saving God."*

Ultimately, **God knows the way, even when you do not.** His plans are not always logical to the human mind, but they are always perfect. Isaiah 55:8-9 (NIV) reminds us, *"For my thoughts are not your thoughts, neither are your ways my ways, declares the Lord."* Trusting God means walking forward, even when the road ahead seems uncertain. **Will you wait until everything makes sense, or will you choose to trust the One who already knows the way?** Proverbs 3:5-6 (NIV) offers this timeless wisdom: *"Trust in the Lord with all your heart and lean not on your own understanding; in all your ways submit to him, and he will make your paths straight."* Faith believes, obeys, and follows not because the way is clear, but because **the One leading the way can always be trusted.**

TRUSTING GOD BEYOND YOUR EXPECTATIONS

Trusting God is easy when His plans align with our desires, but **true faith begins when we trust Him even when nothing makes sense.** Life often brings situations that leave us confused, disappointed, or even questioning God's presence. Yet, the Bible reminds us in Isaiah 55:8-9 (NIV), *"For my thoughts are not your thoughts, neither are your ways my ways," declares the Lord. "As the heavens are higher than the earth, so are my ways higher than your ways and my thoughts than your thoughts."* This verse is a powerful reminder that God's perspective is far greater than ours. **Why should a limited human mind expect to fully comprehend the plans of an unlimited God?** N.T. Wright wrote, "To the child of God, there is no such thing as an accident. He travels an appointed way." God's plans often unfold differently from what we expect, but they always serve a purpose.

Abraham's story in Genesis 22 offers a perfect example of trusting God beyond human expectations. God asked Abraham to sacrifice Isaac, the very son through whom God's promise was to be fulfilled. **What kind of faith does it take to obey God when His command seems to destroy the very promise He gave?** Hebrews 11:17-19 (NIV) highlights Abraham's radical trust: *"Abraham reasoned that God could even raise the dead."* This is faith that does not cling to human reasoning but to God's character. **Could it be that God's unexpected instructions are actually setting us up for divine provision?** In the end, God provided a ram in place of Isaac, proving that trust beyond expectations leads to divine intervention.

In our own journeys, trusting God beyond expectations often means surrendering control over timelines, outcomes, and even our dreams. Joseph's life illustrates this beautifully. Betrayed by his brothers, sold into slavery, and imprisoned for a crime he didn't commit, Joseph had every reason to doubt God's plan. Yet, Joseph trusted God's presence even in the darkest moments. And what happened? God used those very trials to prepare Joseph for a destiny far greater than he could have imagined. What if the delays, detours, and disappointments you face are actually positioning you for something bigger? Proverbs 3:5-6 (NIV) urges us, *"Trust in the Lord with all your heart and lean not on your own understanding."* **True trust means leaning on God's wisdom even when circumstances defy logic.**

One reason we struggle to trust God beyond our expectations is because we assume we know what's best for ourselves. Yet, the Bible consistently reveals that God's plans surpass human imagination. Ephesians 3:20 (NIV) declares, *"Now to him who is able to do immeasurably more than all we ask or imagine."* If God can do far beyond what we ask, why do we limit our trust to what we can see? Andrew Murray wrote, "God is ready to assume full responsibility for the life wholly yielded to Him." Our fear of the unknown often blinds us to the beauty of God's unknown blessings.

Ultimately, **trusting God beyond our expectations opens the door to divine surprises, supernatural provision, and unimaginable blessings.** God does not require us to understand; He requires us to trust. The question is not whether God is able but whether we are willing to trust when life does not go according to plan. **What if the miracle you're waiting for is hidden in the step of obedience you're afraid to take?** Faith means believing that God is good even when circumstances are not. When we trust beyond what we expect, we experience a God who exceeds every expectation with His grace, power, and faithfulness.

GOD DOES NOT WORK ACCORDING TO OUR EXPECTATIONS

It is human nature to expect God to act in ways that align with our logic, desires, and understanding. **We want God to fit into our frame of thinking grand gestures, complex miracles, or visible signs of power.** But God is not bound by human reasoning. Isaiah 55:8-9 (NIV) declares, *"For my thoughts are not your thoughts, neither are your ways my ways," declares the Lord. "As the heavens are higher than the earth, so are my ways higher than your ways and my thoughts than your thoughts."* This truth challenges us to reconsider our assumptions about how God works. **Why should the Creator of the universe operate within the limits of the human mind?** As Hudson Taylor writes, "There are three stages to every great work of God: first it is impossible, then it is difficult, then it is done." When we rely solely on human expectations, we risk missing God's unexpected blessings.

The Bible is filled with stories where people almost missed their miracles because they expected God to act differently. In 2 Kings 5, Naaman, a commander afflicted with leprosy, was offended when Elisha told him to wash in the Jordan River to be healed. Naaman expected a dramatic, prophet-like performance. Yet his healing required simple obedience. **Could it be that many of us are like Naaman turning away from God's answers simply because they look too ordinary?** John 9:6-7 (NIV) recounts how Jesus healed a blind man with mud and water: *"'Go,' he told him, 'wash in the Pool of Siloam.' So, the man went and washed, and came home seeing."* This unconventional method proved that God's power is not restricted to human logic. When God's way seems unusual, do we trust His wisdom or our own preferences?

Pride and doubt are often the biggest obstacles to receiving God's blessings. Pride convinces us that we know better, while doubt causes us to question God's methods. This pattern repeats throughout Scripture. The walls of Jericho (Joshua 6) did not fall because of military strength or brilliant tactics, they fell because the Israelites obeyed God's unusual instruction to march and shout. **Why does God choose such unexpected methods?** Perhaps because simple obedience reveals the condition of our hearts. 2 Corinthians 5:7 (NIV) reminds us, *"For we live by faith, not by sight."* Faith means trusting that God's ways, no matter how simple or strange are always right. Oswald Chambers wrote, "Faith never knows where it is being led, but it loves and knows the One who is leading."

The story of Gideon further proves that God's ways defy human logic. Gideon began with thousands of soldiers, but God reduced his army to just 300 (Judges 7). This reduction was not to weaken Gideon, but to show that victory comes from God, not human strength. **How often do we insist on our own plans, afraid that God's way is too risky?** When Gideon obeyed, God's power was revealed through a victory only God could achieve. This principle applies to us today—whether it is trusting God with our finances, forgiving someone who hurt us, or stepping into a calling that seems beyond our ability. **When we obey, even when it feels illogical, we position ourselves for miracles.**

Ultimately, **trusting God requires surrendering our expectations.** God's methods will not always make sense, and His answers may not come in the packages we expect. But His wisdom far exceeds ours, and His plans are always for our good. 1 Corinthians 1:27 (NIV) says, *"But God chose the foolish things of the world to shame the wise; God chose the weak things of the world to shame the strong."* When we let go of our need to control how God works, we discover the beauty of His unexpected grace. Charles Spurgeon said, "God is too good to be unkind and too wise to be mistaken. When we cannot trace His hand, we must trust His heart." When we trust, obey, and surrender, we open the door to God's supernatural work in our lives, far beyond our imagination and far beyond our expectations.

NOTE THESE

1. God's ways are higher than human understanding, so we must trust Him even when His methods seem unusual.
2. Expecting God to work in familiar ways can cause us to miss His unexpected blessings.
3. Simple obedience to God's instructions, no matter how strange, opens the door to miracles.
4. Pride and doubt can block us from receiving what God has already prepared for us.
5. True faith surrenders personal expectations and fully trusts God's divine wisdom and timing.

GENERATIONAL PROBLEMS NEED A SPIRITUAL SOLUTION

Generational problems, such as cycles of poverty, addiction, broken relationships, and even chronic illness, are often seen as inherited misfortunes. But could these struggles be more than just genetics or environment? **The Bible reveals that some family struggles are rooted in spiritual strongholds passed down from generation to generation.** *Exodus 20:5-6 (NIV) says, "I, the Lord your God, am a jealous God, punishing the children for the sin of the parents to the third and fourth generation of those who hate me, but showing love to a thousand generations of those who love me and keep my commandments."* This reveals a sobering reality some battles are not simply inherited tendencies, but spiritual chains. Yet, it also reveals hope: God's blessings can break the cycle and overflow for generations to come.

While science focuses on genetics and behavioral patterns, **the spiritual realm offers a deeper explanation and, more importantly, a permanent solution.** It is easy to believe that if alcoholism, depression, or divorce plagued your parents, the same will happen to you. But *Galatians 3:13 (NIV) declares, "Christ redeemed us from the curse of the law by becoming a curse for us, for it is written: 'Cursed is everyone who is hung on a pole.'"* This truth is powerful Jesus' sacrifice broke the spiritual curses that threaten to pass through our bloodlines. If Christ already paid the price, why should we live in bondage to what our ancestors struggled with? Neil T. Anderson wrote, "The most important belief we possess is a true knowledge of who God is. The second most important belief is who we are as children of God."

Some Christians, however, fall into the trap of passivity. **They accept generational struggles as their inevitable destiny, assuming that history must repeat itself.** But *2 Corinthians 10:4 (NIV) reminds us, "The weapons we fight with are not the weapons of the world. On the contrary, they have divine power to demolish strongholds."* If God has given us divine weapons, why would we fight spiritual battles with only human reasoning? Are we allowing fear or tradition to silence our prayers? Are we forgetting that *"the prayer of a righteous person is powerful and effective" (James 5:16, NIV)*? Spiritual battles require spiritual weapons and prayer, faith, and obedience are our strongest tools.

Breaking generational problems begins with recognizing their spiritual nature. This does not dismiss the importance of counseling, medicine, or education, but it places **the ultimate solution in God's hands, not human effort alone.** *John 8:36 (NIV) boldly declares, "So if the Son sets you free, you will be free indeed."* This freedom is not just personal; it is generational. When one person in a family breaks the curse through faith and obedience, they open the door for future generations to walk in blessing instead of bondage. Why should your children and grandchildren suffer from the same spiritual chains you had to fight? God's deliverance is not just for you it is for your legacy.

Finally, **choosing faith over fear allows you to rewrite your family's story.** *Isaiah 41:10 (NIV) says, "So do not fear, for I am with you; do not be dismayed, for I am your God. I will strengthen you and help you; I will uphold you with my righteous right hand."* What if you are the one chosen to break the cycle in your family? What if God placed you in your family line not to inherit curses but to end them? When you stand in faith, declare God's Word, and apply His truth, you are not just fighting for yourself you are fighting for generations yet unborn. Stormie Omartian wrote, "The prayers you pray for your children are the most powerful prayers you will ever pray." It is time to rise, break the chains, and pass down a legacy of faith, freedom, and victory.

STOP MAKING LIFE HARDER THAN IT SHOULD BE

Many people live under unnecessary stress because they trust their own wisdom more than they trust God. They carry burdens they were never meant to bear, trying to figure out every solution themselves instead of seeking divine help. But life was never designed to be lived apart from God's guidance. *Matthew 11:28-30 (NIV) offers a beautiful invitation from Jesus: "Come to me, all you who are weary and burdened,* *and I will give you rest. Take my yoke upon you and learn from me, for I am gentle and humble in heart, and you will find rest for your souls. For my yoke is easy and my burden is light.*" Why do we make life heavier than God intended? Why do we refuse to trade our heavy burdens for His light and easy yoke?

Some people believe that receiving God's help should be difficult that salvation must be earned through hard work and religious effort. But **the truth of the gospel is this: salvation is a free gift, not a reward for human effort.** *Ephesians 2:8-9 (NIV) reminds us, "For it is by grace you have been saved, through faith, and this is not from yourselves, it is the gift of God, not by works, so that no one can boast."* Yet how many people still strive to "deserve" God's love? How often do we fall into the trap of thinking that we must fix ourselves before we come to Him? Why not accept this grace instead of making life harder?

Another reason people struggle unnecessarily is because they try to solve spiritual problems with human solutions. When their souls are restless, they seek comfort in possessions or relationships. When anxiety strikes, they turn to self-help books instead of Scripture. But human wisdom can never replace God's truth. *Proverbs 3:5-6 (NIV) advises, "Trust in the Lord with all your heart and lean not on your own understanding; in all your ways submit to him, and he will make your paths straight."* Why rely on limited human knowledge when divine wisdom is freely available? Jonathan Edwards once said, "The enjoyment of God is the only happiness with which our souls can be satisfied." If God holds the answers, why do we so often refuse to ask Him?

Sometimes, God's solutions are so simple that people reject them. **Forgiveness, prayer, and surrender seem too easy to be powerful, but they hold the keys to peace and victory.** Why do we resist praying, thinking it won't change anything? Why do we cling to grudges, assuming that unforgiveness gives us strength? *Isaiah 55:8-9 (NIV) explains why: "For my thoughts are not your thoughts, neither are your ways my ways," declares the Lord. "As the heavens are higher than the earth, so are my ways higher* *than your ways and my thoughts than your thoughts.*" God's ways may not always make sense to us, but they always lead to life.

Life is already filled with trials; why make it even harder by resisting the One who can help? Jesus stands ready to carry what we cannot, to bring peace where there is chaos, and to offer rest to the weary soul. *Psalm 55:22 (NIV) encourages us: "Cast your cares on the Lord and he will sustain you; he will never let the righteous be shaken."* Why insist on carrying what God wants to carry for you? True victory is not found in striving, but in surrendering. As you choose to trust and obey, you will find that life becomes lighter, clearer, and filled with the peace that only God can give. **Stop making life harder than it should be let God lead, and rest in His perfect plan.**

NOTE THESE

1. Trusting God's wisdom brings peace, while relying on your own understanding makes life harder.
2. Salvation is a free gift from God, not something you earn through your own efforts.
3. Spiritual problems require spiritual solutions, human wisdom alone cannot solve them.
4. Simple acts like prayer, forgiveness, and surrender often hold the key to breakthrough.
5. True freedom comes when you lay your burdens at Jesus' feet and allow Him to lead your life.

CHAPTER ELEVEN

BREAK THE CYCLE: STAND FOR YOUR FAMILY

Every family carries a story; some stories are filled with blessings, but others are marked by repeated struggles, broken relationships, addictions, poverty, and spiritual bondage passed down through generations. **These repeated cycles are not just coincidences; they are spiritual patterns that need to be confronted and broken.** The Bible teaches us that we are not prisoners of our family's past. *"Therefore, if the Son make you free, ye shall be free indeed"* (John 8:36, KJV). Jesus offers complete and lasting freedom not only for the individual but for entire households. When one person stands in faith and refuses to allow past curses to continue, they become a spiritual gatekeeper, shifting the destiny of future generations.

Breaking the cycle begins with a personal decision to follow Christ wholeheartedly. **You do not have to accept dysfunction, sin, or suffering simply because it "runs in the family."** Joshua, a leader of Israel, made this clear when he boldly declared, *"As for me and my house, we will serve the Lord"* (Joshua 24:15, KJV). Can one person's faith really change an entire family? Absolutely! Look at Rahab, whose act of faith not only saved her life but also spared her entire household (Joshua 2:12-13). Isn't it time for someone in your family to rise up in faith and declare, "It ends with me"?

But why do so many hesitate to take that stand? Some believe they are powerless because of their family's past. Others feel too weak or unqualified to bring change. However, **God does not look for perfect people; He looks for willing hearts.** Even if your family's history is filled with pain, Jesus offers a fresh start. *"Behold, I make all things new"* (Revelation 21:5, KJV). Why cling to a painful legacy when Christ offers a new one built on grace, love, and victory?

Standing in faith for your family does not mean life will instantly become easy **it means you become a spiritual warrior, standing in the gap for those who came before you and those who will come after you.** Ezekiel 22:30 says, *"And I sought for a man among them, that should make up the hedge, and stand in the gap before me for the land."* Your prayers, obedience, and faith become the foundation for generational blessing. As you break the curses of addiction, poverty, sickness, and spiritual blindness through prayer and trust in God, you create a spiritual inheritance of righteousness, peace, and favor for your children and grandchildren.

Finally, taking a stand for your family is not only about prayer it requires walking in obedience and modeling faith. Your children and loved ones will see your trust in God through your daily life. They will witness you forgive where others held grudges, worship when others worried, and trust God when others panicked. **When you live a life of faith, you leave a spiritual blueprint for your family to follow.** With Jesus, no family story is too broken to be rewritten, no curse is too strong to be broken, and no cycle is too powerful to be stopped. The choice is yours will you be the one to break the cycle?

STAND WITH GOD FOR YOUR FAMILY

Every family carries a unique story some stories are filled with testimonies of faith and blessings, while others reveal painful cycles of addiction, poverty, brokenness, and rebellion. **The reality is that generational struggles often persist because no one in the family rises up to confront them.** But is your family's destiny sealed by the past? Or can one person's faith alter the course of generations to come? The Bible makes it clear that standing with God can rewrite a family's legacy. *"The curse of the Lord is in the house of the wicked: but he blesseth the habitation of the just"* (Proverbs 3:33, KJV). No matter how dark your family history may be, God's blessing can begin with you when you choose to stand in faith.

Taking a stand with God for your family requires **spiritual responsibility** a willingness to cover your loved ones in prayer, just as Job did. *"And it was so, when the days of their feasting were gone about, that Job sent and sanctified them...and offered burnt offerings according to the number of them all: for Job said, It may be that my sons have sinned, and cursed God in their hearts. Thus did Job continually"* (Job 1:5, KJV). Job didn't assume his children would naturally walk in righteousness; he actively interceded for them. How often do we pray for our family members, standing in the gap when they are spiritually vulnerable?

Generational curses and spiritual strongholds do not break themselves. These cycles, whether addiction, bitterness, poverty, or rebellion, persist when they go unchallenged. Paul reminds us that *"the weapons of our warfare are not carnal, but mighty through God to the pulling down of strong holds"* (2 Corinthians 10:4, KJV). Spiritual battles demand spiritual solutions. It is not enough to wish for change; you must fight for your family's freedom through prayer, fasting, and declaring God's Word over your home. Can one voice of faith change a family's story? Yes, because God honors the faith of those who stand on His promises.

However, prayer alone is not enough. **Your life must preach louder than your words.** When you live in obedience to God, your actions testify to the transforming power of Christ. *"Let your light so shine before men, that they may see your good works, and glorify your Father which is in heaven"* (Matthew 5:16, KJV). What message does your lifestyle send to your children, spouse, or relatives? Are you showing them that faith is real, practical, and powerful? As your family watches you forgive, love, give, and worship, they will see that God is not just a belief but a living presence in your home.

Finally, standing with God for your family means making a public and private declaration like Joshua. *"As for me and my house, we will serve the Lord"* (Joshua 24:15, KJV). This is more than a personal vow it is a spiritual banner you raise over your household. **When you make that stand, you invite God's presence to reign in your home, influencing your children and future generations.** The past does not have to dictate the future. When you choose to stand with God, you become the first link in a new chain of blessing, faith, and purpose. What legacy will your family remember? With God, you have the ability to create one filled with grace and victory.

BREAK THE CYCLE OF IGNORANCE AND REGRET

Throughout history, many families have unknowingly walked the same painful paths as their ancestors. **The struggles of one generation often become the inheritance of the next not because God ordained it, but because no one stood up to break the cycle.** Can ignorance really bind a family in spiritual chains? The Bible warns us about this in *Lamentations 5:7: "Our fathers have sinned, and are not, and we have borne their iniquities"* (KJV). Ignorance is not innocence it is a dangerous form of blindness that allows past failures to creep into the present. As Dietrich Bonhoeffer once said, "Action springs not from thought, but from a readiness for responsibility." Until someone takes responsibility for confronting family strongholds, they will remain hidden beneath layers of denial and regret.

One of the most tragic effects of ignorance is the refusal to confront spiritual battles head-on. Some families live in constant dysfunction, broken marriages, cycles of poverty, and deep-rooted resentment because no one before them acknowledged the spiritual roots of these struggles. *"A prudent man foreseeth the evil, and hideth himself: but the simple pass on, and are punished"* (Proverbs 22:3, KJV). What happens when people refuse to see the spiritual danger around them? Can silence today become sorrow tomorrow? Ignoring family wounds does not make them disappear; it allows them to fester and infect future generations.

Generational curses and spiritual bondage thrive in ignorance. Some believe their struggles are purely physical or emotional, but the Bible reveals that spiritual battles often manifest in repeated patterns of destruction. *"Thou shalt not bow down thyself to them, nor serve them: for I the Lord thy God am a jealous God, visiting the iniquity of the fathers upon the children unto the third and fourth generation"* (Exodus 20:5, KJV). This does not mean God punishes children unfairly it highlights how sin's consequences ripple across time. Yet, through Christ, families can choose a different inheritance, one of blessing, freedom, and restoration. Charles Spurgeon once said, *"You are as much serving God in looking after your own children and training them up in God's fear and minding the house and making your household a church for God as you would be if you had been called to lead an army to battle for the Lord of hosts."*

The cost of ignoring these patterns is far greater than most realize. When one generation chooses to overlook sin, bitterness, or brokenness, the next generation often pays the price. *"My people are destroyed for lack of knowledge: because thou hast rejected knowledge, I will also reject thee"* (Hosea 4:6, KJV). Ignorance is fertile ground for the enemy's lies, and Satan loves to convince families that their struggles are "normal" and unchangeable. But what if someone stood up and declared, "This ends with me"? What if, instead of passing down pain, they passed down faith? As A.W. Tozer said, *"A scared world needs a fearless church."*

The time to break the cycle is now. God's promise of deliverance is not just for individuals, it extends to households and generations. *"The righteous cry, and the Lord heareth, and delivereth them out of all their troubles"* (Psalm 34:17, KJV). What you confront today can set your children free tomorrow. **You have the power, through Christ, to rewrite your family's story.** Will you choose the courage to face what others ignored? Will you seek God's wisdom instead of walking in blindness? The change starts with you when you choose to break the cycle of ignorance and regret, you open the door for your family to walk in healing, truth, and generational blessing.

NOTE THESE

1. Ignoring spiritual battles and family struggles allows generational cycles of pain to continue.

2. Taking responsibility through prayer, faith, and action can break these destructive patterns.

3. Spiritual ignorance destroys families, but seeking God's wisdom brings freedom and restoration.

4. The choices we make today directly affect the future of our children and grandchildren.

5. With God's help, anyone can break the cycle of ignorance and regret and establish a new legacy of faith and blessings.

RECOGNIZE AND DESTROY SPIRITUAL DECAY

Spiritual decay, much like physical decay, is a slow and silent killer that often goes unnoticed until the damage is severe. Many people live with unresolved emotional and spiritual wounds, unaware that these untreated issues are quietly eating away at their faith, joy, and purpose. **Just as a neglected wound can lead to infection and death, a neglected heart can suffer spiritual necrosis, leaving a person spiritually numb and powerless.** This decay does not happen overnight; it starts with small compromises, ignoring prayer, tolerating sinful habits, and refusing to confront personal pain. *Hebrews 2:1 (NIV) reminds us, "We must pay the most careful attention, therefore, to what we have heard, so that we do not drift away."* If we fail to recognize these warning signs, we allow spiritual death to set in, and we drift further from God's intended path.

One of the most common indicators of spiritual decay is unforgiveness and bitterness. When people hold onto past offenses, they unknowingly invite poison into their own hearts. Bitterness spreads like rot, affecting every relationship and decision. **How can a heart full of resentment receive the peace and joy God promises?** *Ephesians 4:31-32 (NIV) says, "Get rid of all bitterness, rage and anger, brawling and slander, along with* *every form of malice. Be kind and compassionate to one another, forgiving each other, just as in Christ God forgave you."* Corrie Ten Boom affirmed, "Forgiveness is the key that unlocks the door of resentment and the handcuffs of hatred." Without forgiveness, we remain shackled to our pain, unable to move forward into the freedom God intends.

Another significant sign of spiritual decay is generational dysfunction cycles of addiction, poverty, broken relationships, and spiritual apathy passed from one generation to the next. When families fail to confront these spiritual strongholds, they are often inherited by the next generation. But **are we bound to repeat the mistakes of our ancestors, or can we rise up and declare, 'It stops with me'?** *Exodus 20:5-6 (NIV) states, "I, the Lord your God, am a jealous God, punishing the children for the sin of the parents to the third and fourth generation... but showing love to a thousand generations of those who love me and keep my commandments."* God's promise of blessing far outweighs the curse, but it requires someone bold enough to break the cycle through prayer, repentance, and surrender.

Spiritual laziness also feeds decay, leaving believers vulnerable to every wind of temptation and deception. When prayer, Bible study, and worship become optional, faith weakens and the heart becomes hardened. **If we no longer hunger for God's presence, how can we expect to stand strong when storms come?** *1 Thessalonians 5:17 (NIV) urges, "Pray continually."* Oswald Chambers wrote, "Prayer is not an exercise; it is the life." Without constant communion with God, spiritual decay is inevitable. When the enemy finds a heart left unguarded by prayer, he wastes no time planting seeds of doubt, distraction, and fear.

Ultimately, **no one is too broken for God to restore.** Just as a surgeon removes decayed flesh to save the rest of the body, Jesus must cut away spiritual rot to bring true healing and life. But healing starts with recognition and surrender. *Psalm 147:3 (NIV) assures us, "He heals the brokenhearted and binds up their wounds."* No matter how deep the decay, God's grace goes deeper. When we allow Jesus to cleanse us, spiritual decay is replaced with new life, purpose, and lasting freedom. The choice is ours, will we recognize the decay and seek healing, or will we continue to ignore the warning signs until it's too late?

RESTORATION FROM SPIRITUAL BROKENNESS

Spiritual brokenness is a condition that touches almost every human life at some point a deep sense of emptiness caused by sin, betrayal, disappointment, or personal failure. Many people attempt to mask this brokenness with external solutions such as wealth, success, or fleeting pleasures. But **can temporary fixes truly heal an eternal wound?** *Psalm 34:18 (NIV) reminds us, "The Lord is close to the brokenhearted and saves those who are crushed in spirit."* God does not abandon the broken; instead, He draws near, offering love and redemption. A.W. Tozer wrote, "It is doubtful whether God can bless a man greatly until He has hurt him deeply." This highlights how brokenness, when surrendered to God, can become the very tool He uses to mold us into vessels of His grace.

True restoration begins not with self-reliance, but with surrender. When people insist on fixing themselves, they only end up trapped in cycles of frustration and exhaustion. **Why fight battles you were never meant to fight alone?** *Matthew 11:28 (NIV) invites us, "Come to me, all you who are weary and burdened, and I will give you rest."* Jesus offers rest for the restless, healing for the wounded, and hope for the hopeless. The beauty of God's restoration is that He does not merely repair us; He transforms us. In His hands, brokenness is not wasted, it becomes the very soil where new life and purpose can grow.

Another important truth is that **no one is too far gone for God's restoration.** Many believe their past is too sinful, their mistakes too great, or their wounds too deep for God to heal. But is there any sin too big for the cross? *Joel 2:25 (NIV) promises, "I will restore to you the years that the locusts have eaten."* This means even the time lost to pain, sin, and regret can be redeemed. Corrie ten Boom, who endured unimaginable suffering during the Holocaust, affirmed, "There is no pit so deep that God's love is not deeper still." His restoration is not limited to certain people it is for everyone who turns to Him with a repentant and open heart.

However, restoration is not always immediate or easy. Sometimes healing is a process, requiring us to confront painful memories, forgive others, and trust God even when we do not see instant results. **Can we trust God's timing, even when the process feels slow?** *Romans 8:28 (NIV) reassures us, "And we know that in all things God works for the good of those who love him."* Spiritual restoration is not just about personal comfort it is about aligning our lives with God's greater purpose. As Tim Keller wrote, "Suffering is at the very heart of the Christian faith. It is not only the way Christ became like and redeemed us, but it is one of the main ways we become like Him and experience His redemption."

Ultimately, God's plan for restoration is more beautiful than we can imagine. He does not simply put the pieces back together; He creates something entirely new. *Isaiah 43:19 (NIV) declares, "See, I am doing a new thing! Now it springs up; do you not perceive it?"* The brokenness that once seemed unbearable becomes the testimony of God's grace and power. When we allow God to restore us, we do not just recover we emerge stronger, wiser, and more compassionate toward others who are also broken. **Your brokenness, when surrendered to God, becomes a powerful testimony that brings hope to others.** Will you allow Him to write your restoration story?

GREATNESS CAN OFTEN BE OVERSHADOWED BY HIDDEN STRUGGLES

Greatness, as the world defines it, often focuses on outward success, career accomplishments, influence, wealth, and recognition. However, **true greatness cannot exist fully if it is weighed down by unresolved inner struggles.** Many people who appear successful on the surface are silently battling wounds that the public never sees. *1 Samuel 16:7 (NIV) reminds us, "The Lord does not look at the things people look at. People look at the outward appearance, but the Lord looks at the heart."* This means that God is far more concerned with our inner condition than our external achievements. Famous Christian author and preacher Charles Spurgeon once wrote, "**The greatest enemy to human souls is the self-righteous spirit which makes men look to themselves for salvation.**" Even when we appear strong to others, hidden struggles can cripple our spiritual walk if left unchecked.

One critical truth is that **hidden struggles are not always sins; they can also be emotional wounds, past traumas, or even deep insecurities.** What hidden pain are you still carrying, even while excelling in your career, ministry, or family life? *Psalm 32:3-4 (NIV) states, "When I kept silent, my bones wasted away through my groaning all day long. For day and night your hand was heavy on me; my strength was sapped as in the heat of summer."* This shows that unspoken struggles do not disappear. They slowly eat away at our inner peace, draining our joy and strength. Often, we fear being vulnerable about these struggles because society values strength and perfection. Yet, as Henri Nouwen wisely said, "**Our wounds are often the openings into the best and most beautiful part of us.**" Could it be that your hidden struggle is actually the doorway to deeper healing and purpose?

Even the greatest human achievements cannot erase internal brokenness. Promotions, awards, and public admiration may temporarily mask the pain, but **only divine healing can bring true peace.** This is why Scripture repeatedly calls us to come to God not just with our successes, but with our burdens and brokenness. *Matthew 11:28 (NIV) extends this invitation, "Come to me, all you who are weary and burdened, and I will give you rest."* When we measure greatness by worldly standards alone, we deceive ourselves into believing that outward success equals inner wholeness. But the opposite is often true some of the most accomplished people carry the heaviest invisible burdens. **What if true greatness is not about what we achieve but how we allow God to heal, restore, and transform our inner world?**

Ultimately, **hidden struggles are opportunities for divine intervention.** What if the very thing you've been hiding is the key to your spiritual breakthrough? *2 Corinthians 12:9 (NIV) reveals God's perspective: "My grace is sufficient for you, for my power is made perfect in weakness."* This is the beautiful paradox of the Christian faith: our greatest weaknesses become the very platforms where God's strength is displayed. Oswald Chambers wrote, **"God does not give us overcoming life; He gives us life as we overcome."** Hidden struggles, when surrendered to God, no longer have the power to define us. Instead, they become testimonies of God's grace, transforming pain into purpose and wounds into wisdom. If you are carrying something hidden today, will you choose to surrender it to the One who can heal every broken place? Your true greatness lies not in hiding the struggle, but in allowing God to turn it into victory.

NOTE THESE

1. True greatness is not just about outward success but also about inner healing and peace.

2. Hidden struggles, if left unaddressed, can silently hinder spiritual growth and personal fulfillment.

3. God values honesty and vulnerability, and He invites us to bring our hidden burdens to Him.

4. Divine healing is the only lasting solution for inner wounds, not worldly achievements.

5. Our hidden struggles, when surrendered to God, can become testimonies of His grace and power.

Conclusion

As we come to the end of *Try Jesus: No Other But Jesus*, one truth stands clear, Jesus Christ remains the ultimate solution to the uncertainties, struggles, and questions that plague human existence. From the beginning of creation to this present generation, no earthly wisdom, wealth, or human invention has been able to fully satisfy the longing of the human heart or provide lasting peace. Many have chased after temporary solutions, yet they have found themselves empty and frustrated. The Bible reminds us, *"Unless the Lord builds the house, the builders labor in vain."* (Psalm 127:1, NIV). This book has shown that true fulfillment and restoration come only when we invite Jesus into every aspect of our lives our marriages, careers, health, plans, and spiritual journeys.

The world may promote countless philosophies and self-help solutions, but none can match the transforming power of Christ. *Try Jesus* has highlighted how biblical history, from Noah's time to the present, teaches us that life without God leads to destruction, while life centered on Christ leads to peace, purpose, and eternal hope. Jesus Himself extends an invitation in *Matthew 11:28 (NIV)*, saying, *"Come to me, all you who are weary and burdened, and I will give you rest."* This call is timeless and personal. No matter your background, status, or past mistakes, Jesus is ready to walk with you, guide you, and restore every broken place in your life.

Furthermore, this book is not just a theoretical guide; it is a practical manual for living. Each chapter has offered real-life lessons, spiritual insights, and biblical truths to help you break free from cycles of generational struggles, spiritual laziness, and misplaced priorities. When you choose to try Jesus, you are not just choosing a religious option you are surrendering to the One who holds all power, authority, and love. As *Isaiah 41:10 (NIV)* assures us, *"So do not fear, for I am with you; do not be dismayed, for I am your God."* Through every storm and every season, Jesus remains faithful, able to deliver and willing to show you the way forward.

In closing, *TRY JESUS* is more than a book, it is an invitation to transformation. It calls you to step beyond religious routines and personal struggles, and into a living relationship with Jesus Christ. The message is clear: no situation is too hopeless, no sin is too dark, and no heart is too broken for the healing touch of Jesus. As you have journeyed through these pages, you have been shown that trying Jesus is not a gamble, but a guaranteed pathway to peace, purpose, and eternal life. John 14:6 (NIV) affirms this truth, *"Jesus answered, 'I am the way and the truth and the life. No one comes to the Father except through me."*

May this book serve as a reminder that life's deepest questions and struggles can only be answered by the One who created life itself. Trying Jesus means surrendering your plans, pains, and desires into the hands of a loving Savior who desires your wholeness and salvation. No other foundation can stand the test of time and eternity apart from Jesus Christ. As you put into practice the lessons and revelations contained in this book, may you experience the unmatched peace, favor, and power that come from walking closely with Him.

Finally, remember this: *TRY JESUS* is not just a call for today, but a lifestyle for tomorrow and every day after. When storms arise, when answers seem distant, and when life feels overwhelming, do not hesitate try Jesus again and again. His love never runs out, His power never fades, and His grace is always sufficient. Hebrews 13:8 (NIV) declares, *"Jesus Christ is the same yesterday and today and forever."* May your decision to try Jesus open the door to a lifetime of divine encounters, spiritual growth, and eternal victory. Amen.

References

American Standard Version. Oak Harbor, WA: Logos Research Systems, Inc., 1995. Print.

Anderson, S.W., 2020. *The book of psalms*. Lulu. com.

Angel, R.M.D., 2016. *The Wisdom of Solomon and Us: The Quest for Meaning, Morality and a Deeper Relationship with God*. Jewish Lights Publishing.

Bengtson, V.L., Silverstein, M., Putney, N.M. and Harris, S.C., 2015. Does religiousness increase with age? Age changes and generational differences over 35 years. *Journal for the scientific study of religion*, *54*(2), pp.363-379.

Bishop, A., 2023. *Becoming an ally: Breaking the cycle of oppression*. Routledge.

Blomberg, C.L., 2022. *Jesus and the Gospels: An introduction and survey*. B&H Publishing Group.

Boyd, G.A., 2014. *God at war: The Bible and spiritual conflict*. InterVarsity Press.

Brantlinger, P., 2016. *Bread and circuses: Theories of mass culture as social decay* (p. 312). Cornell University Press.

Bridges, J., 2017. *Trusting God*. Tyndale House Publishers, Inc..

Burgman, M.A., 2015. *Trusting judgements: how to get the best out of experts*. Cambridge University Press.

Chaisson, E.J., 2014. The natural science underlying big history. *The Scientific World Journal*, 2014(1), p.384912.

Chao, T.C. and Zichen, Z., 2022. Jesus and the Reality of God. In *The Chinese Face of Jesus Christ: Volume 3a* (pp. 1300-1307). Routledge.

Church, C. and Th, P.S.F.M., The Effects of Signs, Wonders and Miracles on Faith throughout the History of the.

Church, C. and Th, P.S.F.M., The Effects of Signs, Wonders and Miracles on Faith throughout the History of the.

Cohen, H.H., 2023. *The drunkenness of Noah*. FriesenPress.

Cook, C.C., 2019. *Hearing voices, demonic and divine: Scientific and theological perspectives*. Taylor & Francis.

Cunanan, M.S., De Jesus, R.P., Carbonell, D.B., Pacetes, A.v.c. and Santillan, R.P., 2024. Custodial Shadows: Lived Experiences of Postpartum Mothers Deprived of Liberty Journal of Womens Healthcare & Midwifery Research.

Dawson, C., 2014. *Dynamics of world history*. Open Road Media.

Deifelt, W., 2016. Out of Brokenness, a New Creation. *Eco-Reformation: Grace and Hope for a Planet in Peril*, p.55.

DiAngelo, R., 2022. *White fragility: Why Understanding racism can be so hard for white people (adapted for young adults)*. Beacon press.

Doka, K. and Morgan, J., 2016. *Death and spirituality*. Routledge.

Dowling, E., 2022. *The care crisis: What caused it and how can we end it?*. Verso Books.

Eberhart, C.A., 2018. *The Sacrifice of Jesus: Understanding Atonement Biblically*. Wipf and Stock Publishers.

Eddy, M.B., 2023. *Science and Health with Key to the Scriptures*. BoD–Books on Demand.

REFERENCES

English Standard Version (Esv) The Holy Bible, English Standard Version. ESV® Text Edition: 2016. Copyright © 2001 by Crossway Bibles, a publishing ministry of Good News Publishers.

Falck, C., 2018. The (Re-) Appropriation of Spirit Beings–Spirits of the Dead and Spirits of God in a Sepik Community. *Oceania, 88*(1), pp.107-126.

Ferguson, H., 2018. How social workers reflect in action and when and why they don't: The possibilities and limits to reflective practice in social work. *Social work education, 37*(4), pp.415-427.

Fitch, M.I. and Bartlett, R., 2019. Patient perspectives about spirituality and spiritual care. *Asia-Pacific Journal of Oncology Nursing, 6*(2), pp.111-121.

Foor, K., 2015. *Psalms for Life: A Devotional of Encouragement for the Weary*. WestBow Press.

Fraiberg, S., Adelson, E. and Shapiro, V., 2018. Ghosts in the nursery: a psychoanalytic approach to the problems of impaired infant–mother relationships 1. In *Parent-infant psychodynamics* (pp. 87-117). Routledge.

Gamwell, L., 2020. *Exploring the invisible: art, science, and the spiritual–revised and expanded edition*. Princeton University Press.

Goodwin, B., 2023. *Restoring God: Broken People Can Be Remade by the Restoring God*. WestBow Press.

Hage, G. ed., 2021. *Decay*. Duke University Press.

Harling, B., 2020. *Psalms for the Anxious Heart: A 30-Day Devotional for Uncertain Times*. Moody Publishers.

Heinonen, S., Karjalainen, J. and Taylor, A., 2022. Landscapes of our uncertain Futures. *Towards mapping and understanding crisis-related concepts and definitions. Landscapes of our uncertain Futures. Towards mapping and understanding crisis-related concepts and definitions. FFRC eBooks, 7*, p.2022.

Hout, M. and Fischer, C.S., 2014. Explaining why more Americans have no religious preference: Political backlash and generational succession, 1987-2012. *Sociological Science*, *1*, pp.423-447.

Howes, L., 2023. *The Greatness Mindset: Unlock the Power of Your Mind and Live Your Best Life Today*. Hay House, Inc.

Hubbard, B.M., 2015. *Conscious evolution: Awakening the power of our social potential*. New World Library.

Jesus, I.T.M.D., Orlandi, A.A.D.S. and Zazzetta, M.S., 2018. Burden, profile and care: caregivers of socially vulnerable elderly persons. *Revista Brasileira de Geriatria e Gerontologia*, *21*(02), pp.194-204.

Jibiliza, X. and Kumalo, S.R., 2021. Healing our Brokenness: A pastoral care approach. *Pharos Journal of Theology*, *102*.

Johnston, R.K., 2017. 3 Retelling the Biblical Story of Noah. *Noah as Antihero: Darren Aronofskys Cinematic Deluge*, *9*(6), p.49.

Keating, A., 2020. "I'ma citizen of the universe": Gloria Anzaldúa's spiritual activism as catalyst for social change. In *Feminist theory reader* (pp. 427-433). Routledge.

Kellerman, B. and Pittinsky, T.L., 2020. *Leaders who lust: Power, money, sex, success, legitimacy, legacy*. Cambridge University Press.

Key, A., 2024. *How Intentional Are Saints Who Choose to Live by Faith Receiving and Regarding God's Promises?* (Master's thesis, Regent University).

King, E. and Badham, R., 2019. Leadership in uncertainty. *Organizational Dynamics*, *48*(4), p.100674.

Kinley, J., 2022. *As It Was in the Days of Noah: Warnings from Bible Prophecy About the Coming Global Storm*. Harvest House Publishers.

Knorr, K., 2016. *Power and wealth: the political economy of international power*. Springer.

Kosior, W., 2016. The crimes of love: the (un) censored version of the Flood Story in Noah (2014).

Land, N., 2022. *The dark enlightenment*. Baldwin City: Imperium Press.

Landow, G.P., 2014. *Images of Crisis (Routledge Revivals): Literary Iconology, 1750 to the Present*. Routledge.

Lovelace, R.F., 2020. *Dynamics of spiritual life: An evangelical theology of renewal*. InterVarsity Press.

Lumingkewas, E.M., 2022. Conflict Resolution in Family: Jesus Model. *Klabat Theological Review*, *3*(2), pp.87-105.

MacDonald, K., 2024. The Faith at the End of Knowing. *Religions*, *15*(10), p.1184.

Marcar, K., 2017. In the Days of Noah: Urzeit/Endzeit Correspondence and the Flood Tradition in 1 Peter 3–4. *New Testament Studies*, *63*(4), pp.550-566.

Marshall, R., 2018. Destroying arguments and captivating thoughts: Spiritual warfare prayer as global praxis. In *Prayer and Politics* (pp. 92-113). Routledge.

Neale, M. and Whaley, V., 2020. *The Way of Worship: A Guide to Living and Leading Authentic Worship*. Zondervan Academic.

Ng, W. and Diener, E., 2014. What matters to the rich and the poor? Subjective well-being, financial satisfaction, and postmaterialist needs across the world. *Journal of personality and social psychology*, *107*(2), p.326.

Nicolaus, P., 2018. Noah and the Serpent. *Iran and the Caucasus*, *22*(3), pp.257-273.

Nikolova, N., Möllering, G. and Reihlen, M., 2015. Trusting as a 'leap of faith': Trust-building practices in client–consultant relationships. *Scandinavian journal of management*, *31*(2), pp.232-245.

Pitman, V., 2020. *Unburdened: Stop Living for Jesus So Jesus Can Live through You*. Baker Books.

Punt, J., 2017. Believers or loyalists? Identity and social responsibility of Jesus communities in the Empire. *In die Skriflig*, 51(3), pp.1-8.

Reimer, R., 2024. *Deep Faith: Developing Faith that Releases the Power of God*. Carpenter's Son Publishing.

Rich, K.L., 2017. *The Potter's House: Which Type of Clay Are You?*. Lulu.com.

Rieske, S.M., 2019. *A Tale of Two Families:" This Generation" and the Elect in the Book of Matthew*. Wheaton College.

Riker, W.H., 2017. The nature of trust. In *Social power and political influence* (pp. 63-81). Routledge.

Robeyns, I., 2016. *Having too much*. SSRN.

Robeyns, I., 2019. What, if anything, is wrong with extreme wealth?. *Journal of Human Development and Capabilities*, 20(3), pp.251-266.

Ruel, M., 2017. Christians as believers. In *Ritual and Religious Belief* (pp. 242-264). Routledge.

Scoones, I., 2019. What is uncertainty and why does it matter?.

Sha, L.P., 2019. Jesus—The Embodiment of Peace as the Substance of Faith.

Srinivasan, R., 2018. *Whose global village?: Rethinking how technology shapes our world*. NYU Press.

Sterba, K.R., Burris, J.L., Heiney, S.P., Ruppel, M.B., Ford, M.E. and Zapka, J., 2014. "We both just trusted and leaned on the Lord": a qualitative study of religiousness and spirituality among African American breast cancer survivors and their caregivers. *Quality of Life Research*, 23, pp.1909-1920.

Swift, C., 2017. *Hospital chaplaincy in the twenty-first century: The crisis of spiritual care on the NHS*. Routledge.

Tanzi, V., 2022. *Fragile futures: The uncertain economics of disasters, pandemics, and climate change*. Cambridge University Press.

Taylor, J.E., 2018. What did Jesus look like?.

Taylor, S., 2018. Two modes of sudden spiritual awakening? Ego-dissolution and explosive energetic awakening. *International Journal of Transpersonal Studies*, 37(2), p.11.

The Holy Bible: King James Version. Electronic Edition of the 1900 Authorized Version. Bellingham, WA: Logos Research Systems, Inc., 2009. Print.

The New International Version. Grand Rapids, MI: Zondervan, 2011. Print.

The New King James Version. Nashville: Thomas Nelson, 1982. Print.

Watts, A., 2020. *The two hands of God: The myths of polarity*. New World Library.

Willard, D., 2015. The Allure of Gentleness: Defending the Faith in the Manner of Jesus. Cultural Encounters, 15(1).

Winiarski, D.L., 2017. *Darkness Falls on the Land of Light: Experiencing Religious Awakenings in Eighteenth-Century New England*. UNC Press Books.

Wright, C.J., 2016. *Becoming Like Jesus: Cultivating the Fruit of the Spirit*. Langham Publishing.

Wright, N.T., 2014. *Who was Jesus?*. Wm. B. Eerdmans Publishing.

Wright, N.T., 2015. *The Challenge of Jesus: Rediscovering who Jesus was and is*. InterVarsity Press.

Yancey, P., 2015. *Disappointment with God: Three questions no one asks aloud*. Zondervan.

Yeager, D.S., Purdie-Vaughns, V., Garcia, J., Apfel, N., Brzustoski, P., Master, A., Hessert, W.T., Williams, M.E. and Cohen, G.L., 2014. Breaking the cycle of mistrust: Wise interventions to provide critical feedback across the racial divide. *Journal of Experimental Psychology: General*, 143(2), p.804.

Zaleha, B.D. and Szasz, A., 2015. Why conservative Christians don't believe in climate change. *Bulletin of the Atomic Scientists*, *71*(5), pp.19-30.

Zigan, K., Héliot, Y. and Le Grys, A., 2021. Analyzing leadership attributes in faith-based organizations: Idealism versus reality. *Journal of Business Ethics*, *170*(4), pp.743-757.

Bible References

Psalm 145:3	Proverbs 3:5-6	John 3:16
James 4:14	John 6:35	Matthew 7:13
Hebrews 11:8	Jeremiah 29:13	Ephesians 2:8
Matthew 6:34	John 7:37-38	James 2:26
Ecclesiastes 11:5	Psalm 1:3	Acts 16:31
Ecclesiastes 8:7	Matthew 11:28	Romans 10:9
Matthew 6:34	Amos 8:11	Isaiah 60:2
James 1:2-4	1 Peter 5:7	Matthew 24:37
Proverbs 3:5-6	Proverbs 3:5	Ephesians 5:16
John 16:33	John 7:38,	Ephesians 5:8
Matthew 6:8	Isaiah 26:3	John 8:12
Hebrews 13:8	Genesis 6:5	Matthew 5:14-16
Philippians 4:6-7	Genesis 6:9	Psalm 119:105
Proverbs 3:5-6	Hebrews 11:7	John 14:6
Matthew 6:34	Matthew 24:39	2 Timothy 3:1
Proverbs 16:9	Acts 4:12	John 16:33
Isaiah 41:10	Matthew 24:37	Philippians 4:19
James 1:2-3	John 10:9	Psalm 34:19
Psalm 125:1	2 Peter 3:9	John 14:1
John 1:1	Acts 9:1	Psalm 46:1

John 6:35
Psalm 119:105
2 Timothy 4:3-4
Psalm 119:11
2 Corinthians 6:2
John 4:14
Philippians 2:12
Revelation 22:12
John 7:37-38
2 Corinthians 5:17
Ephesians 6:12,
Colossians 2:15
Ephesians 6:11
John 17:15
Exodus 14:14
John 14:27
Proverbs 3:5
2 Corinthians 5:17
John 16:33
Revelation 3:20
Philippians 2:13
Matthew 11:28
John 10:10
Ephesians 6:12
2 Corinthians 10:4
James 4:7
1 Peter 5:8
Ephesians 6:12

Genesis 6:9
Ezekiel 14:14
Romans 10:13
John 10:9
Hebrews 11:7
Romans 10:9
Matthew 16:27
James 4:8
Matthew 16:27
John 16:33
Ephesians 6:11
Exodus 14:14
Ephesians 5:8
Ephesians 6:12
2 Corinthians 10:4
1 Peter 5:8
John 1:5
Matthew 11:28-30
Psalm 55:22
Isaiah 41:10
John 14:27
Jeremiah 29:11
Exodus 14:14
Hebrews 13:8
2 Kings 5:1
2 Kings 5:11-12
2 Kings 5:14
2 Kings 5:15

Philippians 4:6-7
Isaiah 26:3
Genesis 7:16
John 7:37-38
Matthew 6:34
Psalm 91:2
Hebrews 13:8
2 Kings 5:1
Romans 3:23
2 Kings 5:13-14
John 14:6 (repeated)
1 John 1:9
Ephesians 2:8-9
Mark 8:36
Ecclesiastes 1:2
Proverbs 3:5-6
Isaiah 1:18
Isaiah 59:2
Psalm 34:18
Mark 8:36
2 Kings 5:14
Matthew 11:28
John 14:6
Isaiah 1:18
Ecclesiastes 1:2
Mark 8:36
Proverbs 3:5-6
Matthew 11:28

BIBLE REFERENCES

Psalm 55:22
John 14:27
Philippians 4:6-7
Isaiah 26:3
Proverbs 3:5-6
Jeremiah 29:11
2 Corinthians 5:7
Romans 5:8
Matthew 11:28
Luke 1:37
Exodus 14:21
John 11:43-44
Jeremiah 32:27
Hebrews 11:1
Matthew 11:28
Psalm 18:2
Hebrews 11:6
Mark 5:25-34
Mark 5:28
James 2:26
2 Corinthians 5:7
Joel 2:25
2 Corinthians 5:17
Mark 10:46-52
Mark 10:47
James 4:8
Luke 19:10
2 Kings 5

James 4:10
1 Peter 5:5
Matthew 5:3
Proverbs 11:4
2 Kings 5:13
Psalm 147:3
James 4:6
Joshua 6
Luke 5:5-6
Isaiah 55:8-9
Romans 10:9
Psalm 128:1
Psalm 20:7
John 14:6
Matthew 7:7
Proverbs 8:17
Jeremiah 29:13
Isaiah 61:1
2 Timothy 1:7
1 John 1:9
Luke 10:19
John 8:36
Galatians 3:13
Isaiah 54:17
Joel 2:25
2 Corinthians 5:17
Hosea 4:6
John 10:10

Psalm 119:105
1 Samuel 15
1 Samuel 15:22
Proverbs 3:5-6
James 1:22
John 14:15
Proverbs 3:7
1 Peter 5:7
Matthew 11:28
Jeremiah 29:11
2 Corinthians 6:2
1 Peter 5:7
2 Corinthians 12:9
Matthew 11:28
1 Corinthians 1:27
Hebrews 11:1
Romans 5:8
1 Kings 19:11-12
James 2:26
John 9:6-7
Isaiah 55:8-9
Proverbs 3:5-6
Genesis 22
Hebrews 11:17-19
Ephesians 3:20
2 Kings 5
John 9:6-7
Joshua 6

Proverbs 3:5-6
1 Corinthians 1:27
Hebrews 11:6
John 9:7
John 3:16
Matthew 11:28
Matthew 7:7
John 7:38
Mark 9:23
Isaiah 55:8-9
James 5:16
Romans 10:9
John 9:6-7
John 8:36
Joshua 24:15
Joshua 2:12-13
Revelation 21:5
Ezekiel 22:30
Proverbs 3:33
Job 1:5
2 Corinthians 10:4
Matthew 5:16
Joshua 24:15
Lamentations 5:7
Proverbs 22:3

James 4:7
James 2:26
2 Chronicles 7:14
Psalm 34:17
Luke 10:19
Mark 5:15
1 John 4:4
1 John 3:8
Isaiah 54:17
2 Timothy 3:16
Hebrews 13:8
Mark 9:23
Jeremiah 32:27
John 14:12
Isaiah 55:8-9
Romans 4:20-21
Hebrews 11:1
Ephesians 3:20
Isaiah 55:8-9 (repeated)
Psalm 34:17
Hebrews 2:1
Ephesians 4:31-32
Exodus 20:5-6
1 Thessalonians 5:17
Psalm 147:3

2 Corinthians 5:7
Judges 7
1 Corinthians 1:27
Exodus 20:5-6
Galatians 3:13
2 Corinthians 10:4
James 5:16
John 8:36
Isaiah 41:10
Matthew 11:28-30
Ephesians 2:8-9
Proverbs 3:5-6
Isaiah 55:8-9
Psalm 55:22
Joel 2:25
Romans 8:28
Isaiah 43:19
1 Samuel 16:7
Psalm 32:3-4
Matthew 11:28
2 Corinthians 12:9
Psalm 34:18
Matthew 11:28
Exodus 20:5
Hosea 4:6

OTHER BOOKS BY THE AUTHOR

And many more...

Author's Profile

Nana-Sei Tweretwie is a devoted servant of God with a rich legacy in ministry, spanning over three decades. As the Lead Pastor and Founder of Miracle Temple Assemblies of God in Milton Keynes, UK. He has planted and nurtured several congregations, including Miracle Temple Assemblies of God, Church in Dichemso, a suburb of Kumasi, Ghana, and Bedford, UK and a co-planter of Grace Chapel Assemblies of God in Woking, UK and Faith Assemblies of God Luton, UK. His commitment to spreading the gospel extends beyond church walls. Beyond the pulpit, he serves as a marriage and family counsellor, teaches life coaching and leadership and contributes to missionary leadership across global organisations.

With an apostolic mandate, Reverend Tweretwie has passionately pursued his calling for over 20 years, leveraging every opportunity to share the good news of Jesus Christ. With an MA in Biblical Studies and clear diligence, his global ministry has touched lives across continents, such as North America, Asia, Europe and Africa, bringing salvation, healing, and revival to countless individuals.

Reverend Tweretwie is married to Rev. Mrs Yvonne Tweretwie, and together, they are blessed with five children: Cecilia, Emmanuel, David, Samuel, Joseph, and three grandchildren, Beatrice, Perpetual and Foster. The Tweretwie family is deeply committed to the work of the Lord, actively participating in church and community activities, and inspiring others to live a life devoted to God.

www.ingramcontent.com/pod-product-compliance
Lightning Source LLC
Chambersburg PA
CBHW040108100526
44584CB00029BA/3903